WHAT PRICE INCENTIVES?

WHAT PRICE INCENTIVES?

Economists and the Environment

STEVEN KELMAN
Harvard University

Auburn House Publishing Company
Boston, Massachusetts

Library of Congress Cataloging in Publication Data
Kelman, Steven.
What Price Incentives?

   Includes index.
   1. Environmental policy.   2. Pollution—Economic
aspects.   3. Externalities (Economics)   I. Title.
HC79.E5K4   363.7   81-7883
ISBN 0-86569-082-0   AACR2

Printed in the United States of America

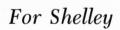

For Shelley

FOREWORD

Why is it that using economic charges to control pollution receives such unanimous support from economists and so little from the rest of us? Is it, as many economists seem to believe, simply that the rest of us are less perceptive? Can't we see how much more efficient a charge system would be than our present regulatory system?

Alas, the question is more complex than mere efficiency. For some time the more skeptical among the rest of us, and some of the more thoughtful among economists, have identified a number of practical problems usually overlooked by proponents of charges.

The impossibility of establishing a "correct" level for such charges has led Professor William Baumol, one of the most respected welfare economists, to conclude that the size of the charge would have to be set by trial and error—not very comforting for a system supposed to promote efficiency. William Drayton, former Assistant Administrator for Planning and Management of the Environmental Protection Agency, has pointed out the vast increase in administrative apparatus implied in an emission-on-charge system: In the vast majority of cases, it would require regular interactions between the government and every single polluter rather than reliance primarily on the credible threat of enforcement to induce "voluntary" compliance.

Now Steven Kelman in his very valuable new book on economists and the environment has elucidated the philosophical reasons for skepticism about using economic charges for pollution control. Seeking to understand why policy makers have shown so little interest in emission charges, Kelman interviewed representatives of environmental organizations and business and staff members of the Senate Committee on Environment and Public Works, which has jurisdiction over the nation's air and water pollution laws. Reflecting on the answers he received, Kelman has produced the first new contribution to the debate over using economic incentives for pollution control in many years, and the only thoughtful critique so far of the philosophical underpinnings of the economists' argument for emission charges.

In stating their preference for the efficiency they postulate for emission charges, Kelman notes, economists are expressing an ideological commitment—one that is not necessarily shared by others in society. For efficiency in the use of resources is not the only social goal. Indeed, efficiency often conflicts with other highly valued social norms—goals such as equity, or fairness, and the desire to promote "altruistic," or unselfish, behavior. The marketplace is the realm of inequality and self-interest, where those with wealth can gratify their desires at the expense of those less well off. The latter may quite reasonably feel skeptical about the expansion of this realm.

The clash between efficiency and other values is particularly evident where public goods such as our political rights or our natural resources are at issue. Kelman writes,

> [P]art of the perceived value of things as varied as our national parks and our right to vote would appear to be their very character as part of a common treasure that we all share equally. . . . Such equal sharing would not occur if those things were placed in the market; it is possible only through non-market allocation.

If the point seems abstract, consider the debate now raging over whether to use "cost-benefit analysis" in establishing health standards for air quality under the Clean Air Act. In line with hundreds of years of the Common Law, the Act now says that every American has the right to an atmosphere that is healthful to breathe. Not efficient, say the economists. An efficient society would apply a kind of market test, cleaning the air only to the degree that the aggregate social "benefits" in improved health were as large as the aggregate costs of providing it. The equity issue hidden in this formula—that the health of some would be appropriated to make cheaper products for others—is of no concern to them.

Though Kelman attempts in one chapter to show economists how they could more effectively promote their case for expanding the role of the market in environmental policy, arguing for or against the economists, ideology is not the primary purpose of his book. What he has done, and done exceedingly well, is explain the social costs involved in applying the test of the marketplace to allocate our remaining common resources of air, water, and land. In so doing, he has reminded us that the real issue involved is not how to become more efficient, but what kind of society we wish to live in.

RICHARD E. AYRES
NATIONAL RESOURCES DEFENSE COUNCIL

ACKNOWLEDGEMENTS

The work on which this book is based was supported by grant #R805446010 from the Office of Research and Development of the Environmental Protection Agency to a group of researchers at the Kennedy School of Government, Harvard University, to study economic incentives and environmental policy. The final report, coauthored by Professors Thomas Schelling, David Harrison, Albert Nichols, Robert Repetto, and myself, was submitted to EPA under the title, "Incentive Arrangements for Environmental Protection: A Critical Examination."

The principal investigator for this team project was Thomas Schelling. I had just completed a doctoral dissertation in the Department of Government at Harvard and was preparing to join the faculty of the Kennedy School of Government the next fall, and Professor Schelling asked me to work on a portion of the project dealing with the politics of economic incentives. Out of that charge came the research and thought that have produced this book. I owe Professor Schelling an enormous debt of gratitude for making the research possible, as well as for his tolerance towards my views on the subject, which diverge fairly significantly both from his own and from those of the other members of the research team (all of whom are economists). Professor Schelling was also generous with helpful comments on portions of the manuscript.

Other thanks are due: to Alan Carlin, project officer at EPA, who helped orient me at the beginning of the project; to Richard Zeckhauser, a valued colleague whose sharp mind has forced me to think more deeply about the nature of our disagreements; to Mark Kelman and Albert Nichols, who read and critiqued sections of the manuscript; to David Bussard and Joan Meier, who worked with good humor and good intelligence both as research assistants and as interviewers for the survey presented in Chapter Three;

and finally, to the sixty-three women and men who gave kindly of their time for our interviews about economic incentives and environmental policy.

STEVEN KELMAN

March 1981   WASHINGTON, D.C.

CONTENTS

WHAT PRICE INCENTIVES?

INTRODUCTION

This book seeks to accomplish two goals. It is a critique of the way economists look at the world when they propose the use of pollution charges or similar economic incentives in environmental policy. It is also a book about people—most of those trained in microeconomic analysis on the one hand, and most of those who aren't on the other—talking past each other when they examine public problems and propose public policies. The relevance, both of the critique and of the fact that some people arguing about public policies are talking past each other, extends, I hope, to other public policy areas where microeconomic theory has been applied.

The system for regulating environmental quality established at the beginning of the 1970s involved setting standards for the maximum levels of pollution that different kinds of sources of pollution are permitted to generate. Sometimes, standards actually specify control technologies that must be installed. The goal of pollution standards, whether they limit maximum emissions levels or whether they mandate certain control technologies, is to achieve certain levels of environmental quality by limiting the sum of pollutants emitted into the air or water.

Economists who write on environmental policy, almost without exception, favor an alternative approach to the way we regulate environmental quality. They believe that, instead of setting standards that forbid pollution emissions above a certain maximum or the operation of industrial processes without certain controls, we should use what they refer to as "economic incentive" approaches. They do *not* mean by this what businessmen generally mean when they talk about the use of economic incentives in environmental policy, namely, subsidies or tax writeoffs for purchase of environmental control equipment. Rather, they mean various efforts to attach a price to pollution so as to discourage

1

its production. The most common proposal has been to set a charge (or tax) on emissions. One might, for example, establish that for every pound of sulfur dioxide emissions a charge of 25 cents would have to be paid. If a pollution source emitted 10,000 pounds of sulfur dioxide, it would pay a charge of $2,500; if it lowered emissions to 5,000 pounds, the charge would go down to $1,250. Some economists have also proposed that instead of setting a charge in advance, an overall level for the sum of pollution emissions be established and the right to emit units of pollution be auctioned off.[1] Economists believe that the use of economic incentives is unambiguously preferable to the use of standards in environmental regulation, because it allows achievement of any given level of environmental quality at a lower cost than a standards-based approach. (Economists also have views on the methods by which levels of desirable environmental quality ought to be determined—that is, that the method ought to be cost-benefit analysis—but these views will not be treated, except incidentally, in this book.)

Economists who think and write about environmental policy have generally been quite upset that the use of economic incentives, which they have been advocating quite insistently for well over a decade in their writings on environmental policy, for a long time made virtually no headway in environmental regulation. (A standards-based approach was adopted during the major revisions of national clean air and clean water laws adopted in 1970 and 1972, and the argument for charges played only a minor role in debates over the further amendments to the air and water laws adopted in 1977.) The failure of arguments by economists for charges to make any headway for so long was especially frustrating to advocates since, in their view, the case for economic incentives stands as a neutral, technical proposition that needs no statement of values to support it beyond the quite uncontroversial one that it is better to achieve a given goal more cheaply than to achieve the same goal less cheaply.

It will be the contention of this book that the question of whether or not to use economic incentives in environmental policy is not simply a technical question, but is also an ideological, philosophical question, and that many noneconomist participants in the environmental debate tend to react to the issue in ideological terms. For some people the word "philosophical" is pejorative, and for others the word "ideological" is. I mean neither word pejoratively, but only to signify broad arguments of a general and conceptual nature regarding what kind of society we ought to create, going beyond issues just of environmental policy. Furthermore, it is most definitely not the case, in my view, that economists are "nonideological" when they endorse economic incentive approaches, while only others are "ideological." Microeconomic theory, like most ideologies, encompasses organizing principles that allow one to understand the world and explain how it works, and prescriptive principles, often connected with the organizing principles, that tell how the world should be ordered to achieve certain goals.

As it happens, since the adoption of the Clean Air Act Amendments of 1977, advocates of economic incentive approaches in environmental policy have made some headway, certainly more than in the past, in getting some versions of some of their ideas adopted. Even this limited version of the economic incentives agenda has aroused some controversy, and the fuller version of the agenda is more controversial still. Failure by economists to recognize the ideological nature of microeconomic theory makes its adherents less able to understand the nature of opposition to the use of economic incentives in environmental policy and to other proposals that grow out of microeconomic theory.

Ideologies are important organizing principles for the stimuli a person receives. The study of perception in psychology and philosophy proceeds from the insight that without organizing principles in the brain, it would be impossible for anybody to make sense of the mass of sensory stimuli assaulting him. Everything would be a mass of light, sound, and smell, and we would quickly go mad. At a preconscious level, organizing principles allow us to assimilate this assault of stimuli into the familiar. The price we pay for this—and it is a small price, considering the psychological anarchy that would ensue without organizing principles—is that we sometimes misperceive things or fail to perceive them at all because they don't fit in with the organizing principles our brains use. Within cognitive psychology, experiments illuminating this insight are common in the study of perception. One experiment showed that people perceived a rotating trapezoidal window frame as oscillating instead of rotating so that the window frame itself could be perceived as being the familiar square shape.[2] In another experiment, people to whom anomalous playing cards (such as a black four of hearts) were flashed tended to assimilate them into familiar categories. "The anomalous cards were almost always identified, without apparent hesitation or puzzlement, as normal."[3]

These preconscious organizing principles exist at the conscious level as well in the form of ideologies, which organize the confusing welter of information a person receives about the political and social world. Ideologies help organize the information and values politically active people need to act in politics. But ideologies too can cause misperceptions or failures to perceive. John Steinbruner, in his book *The Cybernetic Theory of Decision*, uses results from the perception literature in cognitive psychology to help explain the behavior of advocates of a multilateral nuclear force within the State Department during the Kennedy and Johnson administrations. Committed to an ideology organized around the concept of European integration, the State Department multilateral force advocates reinterpreted information they received about European reactions to the idea in the light of the organizing principles of their ideology, interpretations of reality that most people not sharing the ideology would regard as distortions of reality.

Thomas Kuhn's *The Structure of Scientific Revolutions* treats the history of scientific advances in a way parallel to that suggested here. Major scientific revolutions—such as those initiated by Copernicus, Newton, Lavoisier, or Einstein—did not simply involve accretions to knowledge. They mainly involved, in Kuhn's view, the development of a new paradigm, a new set of principles through which reality is organized. Each paradigm not only allows one to answer certain questions, but also directs one's attention to certain questions as being important to try to answer. The process of "normal science," according to one paradigm, involves research in areas where the organizing principles of the paradigm direct attention. As Kuhn notes:[4]

> (T)hat enterprise seems an attempt to force nature into the preformed and relatively inflexible box that the paradigm supplies. No part of the aim of normal science is to call forth new phenomena; indeed those that will not fit the box are often not seen at all. . . . The areas investigated by normal science are, of course, miniscule; the enterprise . . . has drastically restricted vision.

As the role of government in society has expanded, so too have disciplined, scholarly efforts to develop an analytical framework, both for examining public problems and prescribing solutions to them. Interestingly, and perhaps surprisingly, during the last decade, when public policy degree programs emerged at a number of major universities and when the new profession of "policy analyst" was born, economists have come to dominate these scholarly efforts to the extent that, today, when a student in a public policy degree program at a university studies "policy analysis," what he or she is in fact studying is basically applied microeconomic theory.[5] Many people outside academia would regard this development as somewhat surprising, because they are used to thinking about contributions from economists only in public policy areas where the "economic" component is immediately apparent—in making proposals about monetary or fiscal policy, or in estimating costs of various proposals. That economics provides a broader, coherent framework for prescribing public policies in general would, I think, be much less immediately apparent. In particular, it is interesting that political science—the discipline in which governments and what they do are overtly studied—has taken a definite back seat to economics as an endeavor that informs scholarly public policy analysis. (I have frequently heard colleagues who are political scientists express surprise at how small a role political science plays in the curriculum of graduate public policy programs. Their assumption had often been that public policy programs were mere "practical" versions of graduate programs or political science.)

That economics has "won out" over political science as a framework for scholarly analysis of public policy reflects in significant measure the different ambitions of the two disciplines. Political scientists do analyze governments and what they do, but the mainstream of the profession limits itself to explaining why government outputs become what they become—by analyzing why elections turn out as they do, and by explaining processes of decision-making or organizational behavior in the legislative, executive, or judicial branches. Political scientists, then, generally try to explain what government *does* do. Few political scientists try to prescribe what government *should* do, and there is certainly little in the analytical frameworks that political scientists use that would grant them expertise in making such judgments. (Two exceptions should be noted. The analytical frameworks that political scientists use to explain bureaucratic behavior, for example, may be helpful in making prescriptions about what kinds of government policies are or are not likely to be successful in meeting their own stated goals. And various analytic frameworks that political scientists use for looking at international politics are the most important scholarly prescriptive frameworks in that policy area.) By contrast with most of political science, microeconomic analysis provides a framework both for analyzing what kinds of public policies governments ought to pursue and also one that actually crunches out large numbers of definite answers in large numbers of policy areas. Intellectually, economists have had an advantage in gaining hegemony over the discipline of public policy because microeconomic theory explicitly deals, among other things, with the question of what governments ought to do; psychologically, economists have had an advantage because they have been both confident of their answers and united about them.

That a group as large and diverse as "economists" should be united in their answers to important public policy questions probably appears odd, on a number of grounds, to most people who haven't been exposed to work economists have done in such areas as environmental policy. First, as a general point, economists are part of a larger caste called intellectuals, and intellectuals are renowned (perhaps notorious) for their proclivity for argument and debate. Second, the exposure of the typical informed citizen to pronouncements of economists on public policy questions has mostly involved hearing widely discordant prescriptions in areas of fiscal and monetary policy.

In fact, on any number of questions where intelligent people as a whole are quite divided—but where answers to the question may be sought using the analytic framework of microeconomic theory—economists are amazingly close to unanimous. One would be hard-pressed to find an economist (individual examples though there surely are) who does believe that cash transfers are superior to food stamps as a way to aid the poor, that the minimum wage is a bad idea, that cost-benefit analysis should be used as far as possible to determine the appropriate stringency of environmental requirements, or that the price of oil should not be controlled. The quasi unanimity among economists can survive the urge of intellectuals to be contentious both because economists always have noneconomists to debate against (economists are quite capable of unrelenting polemic in such debates) and because there remain economic questions that good microeconomists can still debate among each other. The cacophony of economic prescriptions in fiscal and monetary policy involves conclusions drawn from macroeconomic theory—the theory that seeks to explain the determinants of aggregate levels of economic growth, inflation, and employment. There are, indeed, major divisions at fundamental theoretical levels among competing macroeconomic theories (Keynesian, monetarist, etc.), none of which has definitively established itself among macroeconomists. This stands in contrast to the less controversial (within the profession, at any rate) body of microeconomic theory—a disaggregated theory whose building blocks are the producing and exchanging activities of individuals.[6] And, indeed, the near-unanimity of the answers economists give to public policy questions, highly controversial among the run of intelligent observers, but which share the characteristic of being able to be analyzed in terms of microeconomic theory, reminds one of the unanimity characterizing bodies such as the politburo of the Soviet Communist Party. At the government agency where I have worked and where agency lawyers and agency microeconomists interact with each other on public policy issues the agency faces, the lawyers are often exasperated, not only by the frequency with which agency economists attack their proposals but also by the unanimity among the agency economists in their oppostition. The lawyers often tend (incorrectly) to attribute this opposition to failure to hire "a broad enough spectrum" of economists, and to beg the economists, if they can't support the lawyers' proposals, at least to give them "the best economic arguments" in favor of them, which they could at least use in an adversary legal process. The economists' answer is typically something like, "There are no good economic arguments for your proposal."

The analogy with the Soviet politburo is perhaps harsh; I use it not simply to pique or polemicize, but because I believe it captures something important for understanding the way economists think and for understanding why economists and noneconomists frequently talk past each other when they discuss public policy questions. Students of the ways totalitarian organizations gain unanimity of outlook among followers stress two related points. One is the way the organizations provide members with an ideology that provides many answers to important questions, answers that often are arcane in the sense that they are not apparent to those who are ignorant of the ideology. A second is that the organizations expend enormous effort in socializing people into the ideology, making it an integral part of them. Doubtless unintentionally, the conditions for successful socialization of numbers of people into an ideology that leads them to quasi unanimous acceptance of a particular, somewhat idiosyncratic set of views are reproduced in graduate education in economics. The answers that microeconomic theory provides to public policy questions are indeed arcane in the sense that they are not apparent to those who are ignorant of the ideology. And any graduate educational program involves intense exposure to a set of ideas and a sort of baptism by fire.

All this is relevant to the themes and arguments to be presented in this book. Macroeconomic theory, like political science theory, seeks mainly to explain and predict. As suggested earlier, microeconomic theory is an ideology that provides both organizing principles and prescriptive principles related to the organizing principles. (In Marxism, the theory of surplus value is an organizing principle that purports to help one understand reality as well as a feature of the prescriptive apparatus Marxism develops.) The organizing principles that economists use when they examine the world in order to make judgments about environmental policy lead them to perceive certain things and to fail to perceive others; the organizing principles most environmentalists use to make such judgments lead *them* to fail to perceive some things economists do see while perceiving other things economists don't. Hence the phenomenon of people talking past each other. An environmentalist makes an argument that simply doesn't "register" with an economist; the words are heard but the ideas don't fit in with how an economist organizes reality. The same phenomenon occurs in reverse: an economist makes an argument that fails to register with an environmentalist for the same reason. And, in terms of microeconomics as prescription, it is my conviction that a necessary critique of microeconomics as a normative guide to public policy proceeds by way of philosophical discussion of early premises on which the theory, like ideologies in general, builds.

The argument of this book will proceed as follows. After presenting the efficiency-based case economists make for the use of economic incentives in environmental policy, I will proceed to a critique that examines reasons to be concerned about such a prescription, having to do with the kind of society we promote by acting the way economists recommend.[7]

The views I will express in this critique are my own. However, I believe that they do express, in more abstract or perhaps philosophical form, general beliefs that many noneconomists hold in an unanalyzed or intuitive way. (That these beliefs remain intuitive should *not* be interpreted as a criticism. Those in question presumably have better things to do with their time than to try to analyze their beliefs in these regards!) I believe further that many environmentalists apply such general beliefs to the specific area of environmental policy—an application presupposing a high weight ascribed the value of a clean environment that is less widespread than the general beliefs themselves—and combine these general beliefs with specific environmental commitment to produce a skepticism or uneasiness about economist proposals for use of economic incentives in environmental policy. The second major part of the book will present results of a 1978 survey of Washington-based congressional staff and interest-group representatives on attitudes towards the use of economic incentives in environmental policy. The survey findings, I believe, confirm the view that participants in the environmental policy debate—not only opponents of economic incentives, but supporters as well—have important ideological concerns and that these concerns play an important role in shaping opposition, or support, for economic incentive programs.

This book is primarily aimed at people familiar with, and perhaps sympathetic to, microeconomic prescriptions for public policy. I hope to present them with arguments for why considerations beyond those typically included in microeconomic theory are important in making a decision about whether to use economic incentives in environmental policy, considerations that make the case for such an approach considerably less clear-cut than it otherwise would be. They may or may not be persuaded. But I also hope to show them that, whether or not they themselves find these other considerations important, large numbers of participants in environmental policy formation do, and that they therefore ought at least to try to get inside the minds of noneconomists well enough to understand why economists and non-economists frequently talk past each other. By trying as I will to reformulate what I take to be the feelings of many noneconomists into language that I believe economists can more readily accept than the objections they often hear from noneconomists (and tend to regard as silly or ignorant), I hope to make a contribution towards bridging the perceptual gap.

This exercise should be useful for noneconomists as well. As will be made clear, the organizing and prescriptive principles noneconomists use frequently inhibit them from registering or

appreciating arguments that economists make, and thus from giving them the consideration they deserve. The account to be presented may help bridge the gap from the noneconomist side as
well. Noneconomists can no longer simply ignore the role of academic economists in the public policy debate; the influence is
a fact of life, and, with the Republican administration elected in
1980, it promises to grow rather than diminish. Also, when first
presented economists' arguments, many noneconomists who have
never been exposed to them before, but who nevertheless grasp
them, enter a state of intellectual shell shock. They feel there is
"something" wrong with what the economists are saying, but they
can't conceptualize or articulate it properly. By seeking to conceptualize and articulate the vague feelings, I hope to contribute
to the ability of noneconomists to engage in intellectual dialogue
with economists.

My own view is that the considerations discussed in the first
part of the book are frequently weighty enough for a conclusion
that, on balance, the price system should not be used, as economists propose, to deal with undesirable effects on others of human
behavior. In the specific case of environmental policy, the efficiency advantages of the approach may well be great enough to
make it, on balance, merited. The final section of this book, therefore, approaches the question of the use of economic incentives
in environmental policy from the point of view of the advocate,
albeit an advocate chastened by the arguments and findings presented earlier in the book. The political environment for the debate over the use of economic incentives in environmental policy,
as well as questions of political strategy for the incentives advocate,
are discussed.

The style and presentation of the three parts of this book varies
rather considerably. The first part is an exercise in philosophy.
The second part presents findings—mainly tables and narrative—
of a survey of actual participants in the environmental policy process regarding their knowledge of and attitudes towards the use
of economic incentive approaches in environmental policy. The
third part discusses political strategy from the point of view of a
policy entrepreneur who is trying to get his ideas adopted. Perhaps
an advance disclosure of this fact will serve to diminish the jarring
feeling the shift in styles might induce. The three segments, however, are unified by an overriding purpose of widening the perspective of those who find the microeconomic approach to public

policy questions comfortable or even self-evident, to suggest that there are more things on earth than are dreamt of in their philosophy.

Endnotes

1. The classic statement of the case for pollution charges is Allen V. Kneese and Charles L. Schultze, *Pollution, Prices, and Public Policy* (Washington, D.C.: The Brookings Institution, 1975). See also the contributions in Robert Dorfman and Nancy S. Dorfman, eds., *Economics of the Environment* (New York: Norton, 1972). The notion of setting an overall level of allowable pollution and auctioning off rights to emit is generally referred to as a "marketable rights" approach; it will be discussed only peripherally here.
2. The psychological and philosophical literature on perception and on organizing principles is, of course, enormous. For a good introduction, oriented towards public policy implications, see John Steinbruner, *The Cybernetic Theory of Decision* (Princeton: Princeton University Press, 1974), especially Ch. 4. The experiment I discuss is reported on pp. 89–90.
3. Thomas S. Kuhn, *The Structure of Scientific Revolutions* (Chicago: University of Chicago Press, 1963), p. 63.
4. Ibid., p. 24.
5. See introductory textbooks on policy analysis, such as Edith Stokey and Richard Zeckhauser, *A Primer for Policy Analysis* (New York: Norton, 1978), and E. S. Quade, *Analysis for Public Decisions* (New York: Elsevier, 1975).
6. Note that the facile objection sometimes heard concerning the efforts of economists to prescribe public policies in areas such as the environment— "if economists can't even predict the inflation rate, how can they ask us to believe them about this?"—confuses macro- and microeconomic theory. As a microeconomist colleague once remarked to me, "Macro gives micro a bad name."
7. This critique encompasses only one aspect of standard microeconomic prescriptions for public policy, the view that the price system ought to be used to take account of "externalities" that are adjudged unacceptable. Other important aspects of standard microeconomic prescriptions, such as the view that policies should be chosen to maximize net benefits (benefit-cost analysis), will not be discussed here. For some discussion of this, see Steven Kelman, "Cost-Benefit Analysis: An Ethical Critique," *Regulation*, 5 (January 1981).

Chapter 1

ECONOMIC THEORY AND THE CASE FOR CHARGES

At its simplest and most appealing, the case for using charges rather than standards in environmental policy is simply that it is better to achieve a given objective for less money rather than more money. The objective in environmental policy may be regarded as achieving some level of ambient air or water stream quality. Different sources of a given pollutant present widely differing costs in reducing their emissions by a given quantity. A system of standards means that sources with widely differing cleanup costs must reduce emissions by the same quantity. It would be cheaper to obtain the same objective by using differential reductions for individual sources, so that those for whom it is cheaper to clean up cut their emissions more than the average amount and those for whom it is more expensive cut them less. A system of charges allows this. If firms face a fixed charge for each unit of pollution, they will find it profitable to continue to clean up until the point where the marginal cost of further cleanup equals the charge. Those for whom cleanup is cheaper will continue to find it profitable to reduce pollution a great deal, while those for whom cleanup is more expensive will find it profitable to reduce pollution less.

Few would disagree with the view that if one policy tool can produce certain results at less expense than another tool, the cheaper tool should be chosen. Other arguments for the advantages of charges over standards may be made as well, but, by contrast, they lack either the cogency of this argument or the uncontroversial assent it would receive. It is sometimes argued that charges are virtually self-enforcing, while standards require lengthy litigation to enforce and invite delay. This proposition about automatic enforcement may not be true, because little time has been devoted to imagining what methods recalcitrant industries might use to avoid paying the charge or what the enforcement attitude of the Internal Revenue Service (which, rather than the Environmental Protection Agency, would do enforcement) would be. Even if the contention about greater ease of enforcement were true, one should not simply compare an easily enforced charges regime that has been wished into existence with a standards regime as it actually functions. Presumably, the substantive opposition by polluters to requirements that they reduce emissions, which under a standards regime gets channeled partly into litigation and delay, would in a charges world become channeled all the harder into political action to get the charge set low or to get provisions adopted that would allow litigation and delay. Like a liquid, opposition may fit the form of the container. Another argument for charges over standards is that they encourage technological innovation in a way that standards don't. This contention applies, however, only to specification standards, where the regulatory agency tells industry exactly what it must do to reduce pollution. Such standards do, indeed, tend to freeze pollution control technology. But most EPA standards have been performance standards, mandating a certain degree of pollution reduction, but not specifying how it is to be met. There is still, then, an incentive for technological innovation in meeting the standard. To be sure, there is no incentive for developing a technology that will allow pollution reductions below the standard (unless the standard is lowered). However, given the large degree of pollution reduction most EPA regulations mandate, and the difficulty many industries have meeting even these requirements, this is not a practical problem in most cases.

The Efficiency Argument for Charges

There remains, unassailed, the argument that one may achieve a given level of environmental quality more cheaply using charges than using standards. On the face of it, this argument for charges appears like one that anybody could have conceived, one that is divorced from any larger theoretical construct. In fact, it grows directly out of the analysis in microeconomic theory about the conditions for "economic efficiency." To simplify dramatically, an economically efficient world is one where resources are allocated to those uses that are valued most. Productive resources will be put to use producing those goods consumers value most highly by those productive units in the best position to produce them.

In a free market system, prices consumers are willing to pay for various goods signal to producers the varieties and quantities of goods to be produced, directing production towards the goods people value most highly. Many people attach a value to environmental quality and would thus be willing to pay something to have pollution reduced, just as they are willing to pay for food or clothing. But as long as there is no cost (price) attached to pollution to reflect the negative value pollution has, firms are not signalled to reduce their pollution. By placing a charge (price) on pollution that equals the value people give environmental quality, and letting firms respond to that price in a free market, one will achieve production of environmental quality corresponding to people's wants. And the production will be undertaken by those who are in the best position to produce environmental quality— those for whom it is least costly. The situation is analogous to that occurring for production of any good. When consumers signal producers that they are willing to buy candy at a certain price, those who can produce candy most cheaply come forth to produce it, not those for whom it is most expensive. Those firms for whom it is more expensive to produce candy should be producing something else instead; otherwise their productive capacities are not going to their most valued use. Using standards to achieve environmental quality is thus like saying that both candy plants and steel mills should satisfy the demand for candy. This is not the most efficient use of society's productive resources. It will never happen if candy production responds to price, because candy plants will be able to satisfy demand much more cheaply than steel plants, and steel plants will therefore stick to making steel rather than dabbling in candy.

A price on pollution that reflects the value people attach to environmental quality will, in the context of a free market, translate into an efficient production of environmental quality—the achievement of a production of environmental quality that reflects the value people attach to it, by producers who are in the best position to do so. Producing an efficient outcome as far as environmental quality is concerned thus requires setting the price (charge) on pollution at a level corresponding to the value people ascribe to environmental quality. This aspect of the teaching of microeconomic theory as regards environmental policy will only be dealt with tangentially henceforth. The argument for charges rather than standards in environmental policy mainly relates to putting productive resources to their most valued uses; that is, having those who are best placed to reduce pollution do so, and thus provide environmental quality. The argument that one can achieve a given level of environmental quality using charges rather than using standards will henceforth be referred to as the "efficiency argument" for charges. In principle, the argument that one can attain a given level of environmental quality more cheaply using charges than using standards is one that somebody untrained in economics could come upon by a simple process of logical reasoning. In fact, though, the argument grows naturally out of microeconomic theory—indeed, it simply is an application of a general approach to a specific case.

The Larger Context of Economic Theory

If it were an argument disembodied from a larger body of thought, one growing out of a simple logical exercise such as the one presented at the beginning of this chapter, many of the problems that lead economist advocates of economic incentives and other participants in the debate to talk past each other might well be avoided. Shorn of the excess baggage that economic theory imposes, advocates of charges might more easily understand the objections that others feel, and others might be able to focus on the simple argument about cost minimization itself.

However, this is not the case. The argument for charges in the eyes of economists is embedded in a larger paradigm. This paradigm has too many features to analyze in one short book. I will limit myself, therefore, to noting briefly the aspects of the paradigm that relate most directly to the case for charges and/or to the problems I see with the charges approach.

1. The social institution most practically suited to achieve the efficient outcome that is the object of economists' desires is the free market. People's preferences lie at the base of demand for various goods, and resource endowments lie at the base of supply.

They interact in a free market to produce the prices that in turn give signals that direct resources to their most valued uses. "The market" is thus something that economists value very highly. Note that many people, especially environmentalists, would regard environmental degradation as an example of a *failure of the market;* economists do not. They do not regard such degradation as a failure of the market, but rather as a *failure to have a market.* Air, for instance, cannot, because of its physical properties, be owned. Ownership, which involves the right to use something and exclude others from using it if one wishes, is a precondition for market exchange, since if one can use something without giving up something else in return, one will not be willing to pay anything for it. Were it possible to own the air, a market price for it would develop. Those who valued clean air could pay for it and buy some, excluding polluters from using it as a dump site for wastes that dirty it. Those who wished to use air as a dump site would need to pay a price to buy some. Since air cannot be owned and hence not traded on the market, the anomaly develops that clean air is something that is valued, but to which no price is attached. Those who value clean air cannot give expression to that valuation in the marketplace as they would give expression to the value they give steaks or pleasure boats. Were it possible to have a market for air, none of these problems would occur. Environmental degradation thus is not seen as an example of markets failing, but of a failure for there to be markets. If a market could be made to exist for clean air, things would be fine; the purpose of charges is to establish the results of a market by placing a price on pollution that, ideally, would reflect the value people attach to clean air. It seeks, in other words, to mimic a market arrangement.

2. Beyond the efficiency arguments for free markets, most economists also make a philosophical argument having to do with the value of choice. Markets are based on voluntary exchanges among people. In a voluntary exchange, both parties become by definition better off after the exchange than before, or else the exchange would not have been undertaken. The solution to the mystery of how both can become better off lies in the different values different people give to different things. (If I value having a Big Mac more than having $1.50, and McDonald's values $1.50 more than having a Big Mac, we are both better off if I buy the Big Mac from McDonald's.) In the market we are, to use Milton

Friedman's phrase, "free to choose" what we want to do; the market is a realm of freedom. Indeed, while economists tend in the first instance to emphasize the efficiency-producing advantages of markets, preferring to eschew "normative" judgments about the value of choice and the choice-enhancing advantages of markets, Friedman, for one, states that he would be for a market system even if it weren't efficient because it is the system that maximizes freedom of choice.[1] To be sure, by microeconomic analysis, free choice is related to efficiency, since efficiency involves resources being put to their most valued uses, and by choosing preferred goods over less-preferred ones, individuals help produce such a situation. Still, one may make an argument for charges growing out of the philosophical perspective that standards impose certain behavior on polluters, while charges are preferable in that they leave polluters with a choice about how much to pollute and how much of a charge to pay.

3. The market is able to produce an efficient outcome, assuming that all things people value are priced and exchangeable, even assuming individual self-interest. The traditional view in both religion and philosophy has been to look askance at self-interest, in favor of disinterestedness or altruism. Adam Smith began the process of embedding an alternate view into economics with his demonstration that individual pursuit of self-interest could, in a regime of competitive markets, maximize the social good. To be sure, not all valued things are or can be priced and exchanged. When this is the case, pursuit of individual self-interest does not produce an efficient outcome, because self-interested individuals will seek to make use of valued things without paying to do so. The situation with the air, described earlier, where polluters can use a valued resource as a dump site without paying for it, is an example. Whenever valued things are not priced and exchangeable, self-interested behavior may impose external costs (to use a term from economics with which many noneconomists are familiar) on others. Adam Smith argued that pursuit of self-interest would, in a regime of competitive markets, automatically, without further social intervention, maximize the social good. But that argument breaks down when an individual need not consider the external costs of his actions, in which case an individual's self-interested acts can damage others. If these damages are greater than the gains the acts bring the individual, net social good is not maximized. In such cases, social intervention may be necessary

to maximize the social good. But the general judgment in favor of accepting pursuit of self-interest in organizing social arrangements, instead of trying to combat it, as was the traditional approach in religion and moral philosophy before Mandeville and Smith, remains to influence the choice that economists make about how best to deal with external effects. Placing an appropriate charge on the external-cost-imposing behavior gives those imposing a cost a signal about the existence and extent of the imposition. One can then go back to relying on self-interest to produce appropriate behavior. As a general point, economic theory does allow one to demonstrate the neat, counterintuitive proposition that pursuit of self-interest can maximize the social good, and economic analysis generally assumes self-interested behavior. Economists therefore tend to "like" self-interest as a human motivation. (I am certain many economists will bridle at my using the term "like" to describe their attitude towards self-interest, but I would defend doing so.)

4. Economists tend to be rather indifferent towards and radically nonjudgmental about what preferences people have. To most economists, as to the eighteenth-century British philosopher Bentham, "the amount of pleasure being equal, pushpin"—a mindless game popular at the time—"is as good as poetry." Whatever people believe in, like, or dislike seems to be pretty much all right with economists; certainly it is not an object of their professional attention. Economics as a discipline is explicit about its inability to contribute anything to discussions of what preferences people ought to have. Furthermore, proofs of propositions regarding the ability of competitive markets to achieve efficient outcomes depend on the assumption that the individual is the best judge of his own welfare, and thus that individual preferences be taken as givens. If we do not accept individual preferences, the choices that grow out of them cannot necessarily be regarded as directing resources to the uses that are most valued, if by "valued" we mean those that will best promote the welfare of those concerned under the circumstances. We could still say that markets direct resources into those uses that people value the most, but without a correlation between what people do value and what promotes their welfare, the proposition would be deprived of much significance. It should be noted, then, that economists' lack of interest in what preferences people have and their radical nonjudgmentalism about people's preferences flow logically neither from the

inability of economics to say anything as economics about preferences nor from the requirements for mathematically deduced conclusions about conditions for the maximization of social welfare. But adopting such a stance does allow economists to claim more for the real-world value of their professional tools than would be the case otherwise. Economists would agree that individual behavior that does not take its effects on others into account—such as polluting behavior without a charge that reflects its social costs—is inappropriate. Indeed, that is why economists favor placing a charge on pollution in the first place. But if a charge is set at a level that does reflect the full social cost of the behavior in question, economists' nonjudgmentalism returns in full force. If the charge is paid, few economists would express any criticism of a person undertaking the behavior.

5. Economists, whose theory is based on production and exchange among individuals, have tended to side with those who, following Bentham, were skeptical of the concept of "society," at least as anything more than a sum total of individuals. Economists define "social welfare," for instance, as the sum of individual welfares. Given this skepticism, economic theory was relatively slow to assimilate the notion that people's preferences could include "preferences about society"—that is, views about what the society around them should be like—as well as the other kinds of preferences that economists have been quick to recognize. Recently, some work by economists has recognized the possible existence of preferences about society, although the work tends to talk about preferences individuals may have about the welfare of other *individuals*, rather than talking about preferences about a state of society.[2]

6. Economic analysis has traditionally dealt mainly with material goods. At the root of the economic analysis of consumer behavior are the feelings going on inside people's heads that are at the basis of preferences, but economic analysis has dealt with the revelation of those preferences in terms of behavior rather than with the feelings themselves. Implicit—and often explicit—in arguments for economic incentives is the view that what we should care about in environmental quality is results. What we shouldn't care about, by contrast, is thoughts going on inside people's heads, both inside the heads of polluters when they make decisions about how much to pollute and inside the heads of citizens when they decide how to judge polluters. Interestingly, this concern about

results and not thoughts is a perspective neoclassical economics shares with Marxism. It is possible to extend economic analysis to feelings or emotions, treating these as "goods" analogous to oranges or lamp bulbs—indeed, economic analyses of love, friendship, and other such matters have done just that. But such efforts lie somewhat at an embarrassed periphery of economic analysis, and it is probably fair to say that economists feel more comfortable confining themselves to material goods, although in principle the analyses can be extended to valued feelings as well as valued material goods.

Literature by Economists Supporting Charges in Environmental Policy

Pollution, Prices, and Public Policy by Allen Kneese and Charles Schultze, and Schultze's own *The Public Use of Private Interest* have been the two most widely read arguments for the use of economic incentives for environmental policy in particular and for public policy to deal with the external effects of individual behavior in general.[3] The collection of essays edited by Robert and Nancy S. Dorfman, *Economics of the Environment*, has also been widely read.[4] Kneese, an environmental economist, has testified over the years at congressional hearings, spoken repeatedly with the staff of Senator Peter Domenici (from Kneese's home state of New Mexico and a member of the Senate's environmental affairs subcommittee), and made himself a relatively well-known figure among environmental policymakers in Washington. Schultze was director of the Bureau of the Budget under Lyndon Johnson and became, over the years, a well-known figure among Democratic economists. He served as chairman of the President's Council of Economic Advisors under President Carter.

It is striking, in examining these three books, to note how much their emphasis differs. In the case for economic incentives that Kneese and Schultze make in *Pollution, Prices, and Public Policy*, efficiency arguments hold pride of place. The authors do argue that charges will be easier to enforce than standards and that they promote technological innovation. There is also a brief section entitled "The Broader Problem of Incentives" where the authors note that in government policy "little effort is put into devising new incentives or correcting existing ones to spur individual decision-makers, in their own self-interest, toward socially desirable actions."[5] But most of the book deals, not with any broader issues involved in the use of economic incentives in environmental policy, but with the unnecessary costs that a standards approach imposes. In introducing "the basic economics of pollution control," the authors note right off that one of the "basic facts" about the economics of pollution is that:[6]

> the costs of pollution control vary substantially from . . . firm to firm. To be efficient, the degree by which individual sources have to reduce their pollution discharges should vary. . . .

In the course of the book, Kneese and Schultze present a fairly detailed exposition, in language familiar to noneconomists, of why charges allow attainment of a given degree of environmental quality at a lower cost than standards.[7] The authors present estimates of potential cost savings achievable through allowing differential reduction across sources and conclude that "the difference between inefficient and efficient control policies can mean scores, perhaps hundreds, of billions of dollars released for other useful purposes over the next several decades."[8]

The essays in *Economics of the Environment* are also generally quite narrowly and technically based. Unlike *Pollution, Prices, and Public Policy*, there are also a number of essays that present an analysis of the reasons for pollution in terms of a failure to have markets for air and water.

Schultze's own *The Public Use of Private Interest*, based on his 1976 Godkin lectures at Harvard, deals not just with environmental policy but in a more general way with the various regulatory and other policies governments use to change the behavior of citizens. By contrast with both *Pollution, Prices, and Public Policy* and with the essays in *Economics of the Environment*, Schultze's case draws more broadly a wider microeconomic ideology. His title summarizes the thrust of the argument. "The basic theme of this book," Schultze writes, "is that there is a growing need for collective influence over individual and business behavior that was once the domain of purely private decisions." This is because, in a complex society, the external effects of our behavior increase as our interactions with one another increase. But, Schultze continues, "as a society we are going about the job in a systematically bad way" because, "instead of creating incentives so that public goals become private interests, private interests are left unchanged and obedience to the public goals is commanded."[9]

The Public Use of Private Interest removes efficiency from the head of the parade where it stood in *Pollution, Prices, and Public Policy.* The word "efficiency" appears, scattered throughout the text. But Schultze never presents an argument coherent to someone who did not already understand what he was talking about that explains why economic incentive methods are capable of achieving a given goal at less cost than the "command and control" regulation he criticizes. Indeed, Schultze's discussion of the advantages of the market as a form of social organization excludes efficiency entirely. It is mentioned only as a dependent clause in a sentence beginning, "Quite apart from the maximizing characteristics elaborated in formal economic theory. . . ."[10] Instead, Schultze's case for the market is predominantly a philosophical or ideological one. "Harnessing the 'base' motive of material self-interest to promote the common good," Schultze writes, "is perhaps *the* most important social invention mankind has yet achieved." It might be nice if human activity could be organized on other principles, Schultze continues; but, "however vital they may be to a civilized society, compassion, brotherly love, and patriotism are in too short supply to serve as substitutes."[11] The advantage of arrangements that can turn self-interest into social advantage is that they make use of a motivation the supply of which is not subject to doubt. They are thus more likely to achieve the desired results than are arrangements relying on other motivations:[12]

> *If I want industry to cut down on pollution, indignant tirades about social responsibility can't hold a candle to schemes that reduce the profits of firms who pollute. If I want drivers to economize on gasoline usage, advertising appeals to patriotism, warnings about the energy crisis, and "don't be fuelish" slogans are no match for higher prices at the gas pumps.*

What is needed is not moral condemnation, but changes in incentive systems:[13]

> *In most cases the prerequisite for social gains is the identification, not of villains and heroes, but of the defects in the incentive system that drive ordinary decent citizens into doing things contrary to the common good.*

The second pillar of Schultze's philosophical case for the market consists of the judgment that markets offer people greater choice than do government commands. "While some element of coercion is implicit in any social intervention," Schultze writes, "the use of market-like incentives to achieve public purposes minimizes that element."[14] In his discussion of the advantages of market arrangements, the first one Schultze enumerates is that it is "a form of unanimous-consent arrangement." Government decisions, by contrast, "necessarily (imply) some majority who disapprove of each particular decision." Market arrangements thus "minimize the need for coercion as a means of organizing society."[15] The most sustained efficiency-related discussion in Schultze's book involves the difficulty government has gathering sufficient information about complex problems involving huge numbers of citizens in order intelligently to be able to formulate regulations to change behavior. Yet even this argument is couched in terms of greater freedom to choose. We worry about the relationship between educational inputs and learning outputs, and gather lots of information to try to answer such questions, Schultze argues, because education is not sold on the market. We need not do the same, he continues, with recreation. "Because individuals can choose freely, the prices that millions of them are willing to pay reflect the values they put on various forms of recreation."[16] Free choice based on individual valuations determines the level and mix of recreation production, rather than a political decision that in turn requires costly information search to gather.

For the remainder of the discussion in this book, the efficiency argument for charges will be accepted as correct. In fact, I have no reason to believe that it is false. Thus, it will be accepted as demonstrated that it would indeed be possible to obtain a given level of environmental quality more cheaply using charges than by using standards. I will proceed to examine what reasons might exist to worry about the use of economic incentives in environmental policy even while recognizing that they are a cheaper way to attain a given level of environmental quality. It will become apparent that these reasons relate to some of the broader features of microeconomic ideology to which I have briefly alluded in this chapter.

Endnotes

1. Personal communication with Milton Friedman.
2. See, for instance, H. M. Hochman and J. D. Rogers, "Pareto Optimal Redistribution," *American Economic Review* (September 1969).
3. Allen V. Kneese and Charles L. Schultze, *Pollution, Prices, and Public Policy* (Washington: The Brookings Institution, 1975), and Charles L. Schultze, *The Public Use of Private Interest* (Washington: The Brookings Institution, 1977).
4. Robert and Nancy S. Dorfman, *Economics of the Environment: Selected Readings* (New York: Norton, 1972).
5. Kneese and Schultze, op. cit., p. 7.
6. Ibid., p. 19.
7. Ibid., pp. 85–91.
8. Ibid., p. 83.
9. Schultze, op. cit., pp. 5–6.
10. Ibid., p. 16.
11. Ibid., p. 18.
12. Ibid.
13. Ibid.
14. Ibid., p. 6.
15. Ibid., pp. 16–17.
16. Ibid., p. 19.

Chapter 2

ETHICAL THEORY AND THE CASE FOR CONCERN ABOUT CHARGES

I believe that it is justified to be hesitant about the use of economic incentives in environmental policy out of concerns about the *kind of society we help create* when we choose to change over to doing so. These concerns are of four types:

1. If a society uses economic incentives in environmental policy, it makes a social statement of indifference towards the motives of polluters in reducing pollution. If people may justifiably care about the motives others have for behaving as they do, and if one further believes that using economic incentives endorses self-interested behavior that one may not in the circumstances wish to endorse, then one has reason to be concerned with using economic incentives in environmental policy.

2. If a society uses economic incentives in environmental policy, it fails to make a statement stigmatizing polluting behavior. If one believes that people may justifiably wish the societies they live in on occasion to make approbatory or stigmatory statements about certain behaviors, and if one further believes that polluting behavior should be stigmatized, then one has reason to be concerned with using economic incentives in environmental policy.

3. Using economic incentives in environmental policy means bringing environmental quality into a system of markets

and prices of which it previously has not been a part. If one believes that people may justifiably oppose incorporating some additional previously unpriced but valued things into a system of prices and markets, and if one further believes that environmental quality is something that should not be so incorporated, then one has reason to be concerned with using economic incentives in environmental policy.

4. Frequently, although *not* specifically in the special case of the use of charges in environmental policy, economic incentive approaches produce a situation where wealthier people choose to pay the charge and continue behaving as before, while poorer people, to avoid the charge, are the ones to change their behavior. If one believes that equity considerations may justifiably play a role in the choice of policy instruments in specific policy areas, then one has reason to be concerned with economic incentive approaches that change the behavior of those who are worse off, while those who are better off continue to behave as before.

Implications of Economic Incentives

These concerns have not generally been discussed by economists advocating using economic incentives in environmental policy because the organizing principles according to which microeconomics as ideology channels the perceptions of economists tend to make them insensitive to their existence. They are part of reality, but those using microeconomics to organize reality may not "see" them. To those who do see them, their existence constitutes, to use the language of Thomas Kuhn in *The Structure of Scientific Revolutions,* an anomalous finding that may point to problems with the paradigm as an organizing principle. The failure to be sensitive to such concerns in the area of environmental policy may be generalized to be the existence of blind spots about these types of concerns in other areas where microeconomic theory is used to derive policy prescriptions as well. My own view is that these types of concerns are rather widely shared, by contrast, among people who are not economists. Lots of people frequently would wish to praise or stigmatize certain behavior by others, and to wish to see the societies they live in do the same. Lots of people feel uneasy when talk of putting a price on previously nonmarket things comes up. Lots of people care about whether social actions in specific policy areas are equitable or not. The special regard with which environmentalists hold the quality of the environment is not as widely held. It is the combination of these generally widely held concerns with the specially high weight that environmentalists attribute to environmental quality that combine to produce concern among environmentalists about economic incentive approaches.

I am conceptualizing here in relatively abstract terms reactions that often are presented in intuitive form. People are not forced to analyze these intuitions unless faced with challenges to them, and few people ever get challenged unless they have dealt on a sustained basis with economists who indeed appear to believe, for instance, that it *would* be good if markets were used to steer the production and allocation of everything. James Tobin has noted that "any good second-year graduate student in economics could write a short examination paper proving that voluntary transactions in votes would increase the welfare of the sellers as well as the buyers."[1] Richard Posner, an advocate of the application of economic theory to legal analysis, has himself made a case for permitting a market in babies.[2] Most people have never heard such cases; they have only an intuition that something is dreadfully, and perhaps disgustingly and shockingly, wrong with such proposals. Intuitions have largely remained unanalyzed, then, because most people have never had to analyze them, and because most economists, who might have had to, never shared the intuitions in the first place. The second reason why these themes have found so little place in the thinking of economists is that they have rarely been presented using terms and a conceptual framework with which economists can easily identify. An attempt will therefore be made here to analyze these four areas of concern in terms that either are rephrased from concepts familiar from the microeconomic paradigm or in terms that explain why a certain concern falls outside the areas of attention towards which economic analysis directs people, even though the concern might well be regarded as a fit object for attention.

First, it should be noted that common to these concerns is an importance attributed to thoughts going on inside people's heads. A person who cares about the motives of others in behaving the way they do cares not only about how much pollution potential polluters decide to create, but also about what is going on inside their heads when they make such decisions. A person who cares about whether society stigmatizes polluting behavior cares not only about how much pollution is created, but also about having the opportunity to experience such stigmatization and about what is going on inside the heads of citizens when they decide how to judge polluters. A person who cares about whether environmental quality, previously unpriced and untraded in the market, becomes assimilated into a system of prices and markets, also cares about the diminution of certain positively valued feelings associated with nonmarket relationships and with the down-valuation in the perceived value of certain things when a price is placed on them. Finally, although many arguments can be made regarding the applicability of equity considerations to individual programs, the key arguments I will be making also relate to things going on inside people's heads. A decision to fail to allow equity concerns to be reflected in the design of individual programs has an impact on the ideas people develop about the importance of equity in social life. Sprinkled throughout this chapter will be various arguments about why concern about what goes on inside people's heads is important.

This concern about what goes on inside people's heads contrasts with the behavior and results-oriented approach of economic theory. Yet certainly such a concern corresponds to the everyday experience of most people. Those parts of life that involve simple feelings, without any material goods associated with them, constitute an important part of what makes people happy or unhappy—whether we are praised or condemned, respected or ignored, loved or unloved, laughed with or laughed at.

First, caring about what goes on inside people's heads reflects an *interest in what preferences people have and a concomitant interest in the process of preference formation* (since, if we care what preferences people have, we are likely to care about the processes that produce preferences). Second, caring about what goes on inside people's heads reflects a *concern about the existence and continued production of certain valued feelings*. The explicit refusal of economists to worry about what preferences people have and about the process of preference formation makes them insensitive to arguments that hinge on preferences or influences on the process of preference formation. The greater ease with which economists analyze material goods makes them less receptive to arguments based on concerns over the production of simple feelings, unrelated to any material goods. Economists will be in a better position to understand worry about economic incentive approaches if they see its basis in one phenomenon that their analysis explicitly ignores—a concern with what preferences people have and with the process of preference formation—and in another phenomenon—valued feelings—that they could incorporate into their analysis (there is no reason why feelings cannot be valued as well as goods) but traditionally have been slow to do.

It should also be noted that common to the four concerns expressed above is the view that "society" is a reality. "Society" is a reality not in some mystical sense, but, first, because people's preferences and behaviors are influenced by what they experience around them. It is more likely that a person will believe x or behave in y way if everybody around him does so than if only one percent of everybody around him does so. The sum of individual beliefs or behaviors not only determines the simple distribution of beliefs and behaviors in society, as the individualist view of society would have it, but that distribution at time t in turn influences individual beliefs and behaviors at time $t + 1$. Such a conclusion is probably the single most basic finding of the voluminous research within sociology on the behavior of groups. Political science evidence on voting behavior indicates as well that people with certain characteristics are more likely to vote a certain way if there are many people with similar characteristics around them than if there are few such people; workers who live in areas where mostly workers live are more likely to vote for labor parties than those living where few other workers live.

Society is also a reality because it is one source of the production of feelings that an individual values or disvalues and one unit of analysis for certain moral judgments. Other specific individuals clearly have an impact on whether we experience various valued or disvalued feelings such as love or rejection. But experiencing these feelings can also depend on how widespread a certain attitude is in society as a whole. Hence the development of "preferences about society." For a person who wishes to live in a society with a high level of patriotism or altruism, society is the relevant unit of analysis. Furthermore, for certain moral judgments about relationships among people, such as judgments about the distribution of wealth, the respect accorded various human rights, or the method for reaching social decisions (democratic or dictatorial), society is the appropriate unit of analysis.

For both these reasons, many people may have a concern about what goes on in society. The simple view of society as a sum of individuals is unlikely to capture the concern many people have about "what goes on in society" as an influence on the beliefs, behaviors, feelings, and judgments of individuals.

Caring About Motives

Polluters may have differing motives for decisions to reduce pollution. They may do so out of a belief that they ought to abide by the law. They may do so out of a belief that they should not harm others. They may do so out of a desire to save money by reducing pollution so as to avoid a larger tax payment. Through a decision that endorses self-interest in achieving environmental policy goals, society makes a statement, both to polluters and to citizens in general, that people's motivations in behaving how they do are a matter of indifference. One may be concerned about the use of economic incentives in environmental policy because one does not wish to see such a statement made.

As previously noted, advocates of economic incentives suggest that we should care about what kind of environmental quality, at what cost, various policies produce—and not what motives polluters have in making decisions about how much to reduce pollution. Since charges produce better results than standards, we should be for them. (Over and above an argument that simply expresses indifference about motivations is the psychological "pro self-interest" attitude of economists that I noted earlier.)

The view that we ought to care only about results seems sensible at first blush. Isn't how clean the air and water are, and how much it costs to get them that way, what we care about? In fact, it appears that to suggest otherwise is either to engage in naive sentimentalism or to indulge the professional bias lawyers have for legal edicts that command duties and prohibitions.

I would suggest, however, that what initially may appear to be sensible in fact may be less so. Certainly, the view that we shouldn't care about what motivates people to act as they do is inconsistent both with elements of our legal system and with commonly held views that ordinary people hold. We frequently care about motivations for two reasons. First, bad motivations often tend to produce bad results, when a series of cases is ob-

served. Second, good motivations tend to produce positively valued feelings in those who experience the good motivations. The
first of these two arguments for caring about motivations can (and
in this discussion, to an extent, will) be phrased in terms consistent
with microeconomic theory, although it represents considerations
not typically examined.[3] The second argument, about good motivations producing valued feelings, removes one further from the
ways economists normally think, although again I believe that the
argument can be expressed in terms that will make it more understandable to economists.

As noted, the view that it is results rather than motivations that
matter may sound sensible, even self-evident, until confronted
with counterexamples. We may begin with some given by Charles
Fried:[4]

> *(1) I plunge a dagger into a person's heart. Or I make a decision
> to revalue my country's currency with the foreseeable result that
> my country's wheat crop will be more expensive and the further
> foreseeable result that a person in a distant land will die of hunger.
> Is there any moral difference between the two actions?*
>
> *(2) I am engaged in target practice on private property with
> proper safeguards, but there is still a small chance that someone
> will be hit by a ricocheting bullet. This indeed occurs, and the
> person is killed. Or I want to kill a person, but the only opportunity
> open to me is to shoot at him from a great distance. The chances
> of my hitting him are as low as the chances of an accident in the
> first instance, but contrary to all expectations, I succeed and kill
> him. Is there any moral difference between the two actions?*

The clearest examples of how the legal system takes account
of motivation are seen in criminal law. A person may behave in
a given way, and his behavior may produce a given result; depending on the actor's motivation, he may or may not be convicted
of a crime. (Richard Posner notes that "the subjective intentions
of the accused criminal are a pervasive consideration in the criminal law" and goes on to observe, "This is puzzling to the economist: one can read dozens of books on economics without en-
countering a reference to 'intent.' "[5] Posner, however, does not
regard the lack of attention economists give the subject to be a
shortcoming on their part; instead, his attitude appears to be that
those raising considerations economists do not treat need to give
account of themselves for their insolence by interpreting such
considerations in ways an economist can identify with. It is an
interesting comment on the effect of exposure to the microeco-

nomic paradigm that it makes people with postgraduate training find "puzzling" certain phenomena for which the average person would have relatively little difficulty giving a plausible, and probably not incorrect, account.)

The general requirement in the criminal law is that *mens rea* (criminal intent) is necessary for an act to be a crime. A given statement that one individual makes to another may constitute fraud or it may be no crime at all, depending on the individual's intent in making the statement—even though, in both cases, the statement produced the same unfortunate results for the person to whom it was made. A given killing may constitute homicide, manslaughter, or no crime at all, depending on whether it was premeditated, undertaken in the heat of passion, or accidental— even though, in each case, the person killed is equally dead.[6] If I sell a gun to a person who commits a criminal act, I may share criminal guilt, depending on my motivation in the sale—if I knew he was going to commit a crime with the gun, I am guilty, and if I didn't, I'm not. Indeed, there are crimes, such as conspiracy, that require no overt act at all, but consist only of criminal intention. Furthermore, to *attempt* a crime is itself criminal, even though the attempt fails and produces no results.[7]

There is a link between these aspects of criminal law and everyday morality. To call something a "lie" requires intent to misrepresent; the same false statement might or might not be regarded as a lie, depending on the motivation of the speaker. The same is the case for the everyday meaning of "murder."

The most obvious reason to care about bad motives should be immediately apparent from reflecting on the examples above. We care about bad motives because bad motives tend to produce bad results over a series of cases. It is impossible, therefore, simply to look at one case and say, "We don't care about motives, as long as the results are the same." Although there may be no difference between the results *in the individual case* of the person who tells a lie with intent to defraud and the one who misleads another without intending to do so—or between the case of the unfortunate target shooter and the fiendishly lucky murderer—the behaviors of the well-intentioned and badly intentioned individuals will tend to produce different results *across a universe of cases*. A person who intends to murder others is more likely to accomplish murders than one who doesn't. A person who intends to defraud is more likely to mislead than one who doesn't. By looking at results over a universe of cases, we are only following the injunction of utilitarians to consider the consequences of an act not only narrowly but also for its implications over a universe of results. This is in no way inconsistent with microeconomic theory, though it is a path of analysis that economists who advocate use of economic incentives do not appear to pursue. If the actions of people in whose personalities the motives of lawabidingness or concern for others are important parts tend to produce better results than the actions of people in whom the motive of self-interest nearly always dominates, then there are grounds for caring about the motives polluters have in making decisions about pollution reduction. This is because different motives have different implications for a range of results beyond pollution control.

The reminder that we want to worry about motives because of their implications for a universe of results beyond the results in the individual case is an important emendation to the simple view that "we care about results, not motivations." But there is another broad category of reasons for being concerned with motives. It involves the positively valued feelings associated with good motives. The person who is the object of another's actions frequently feels differently about two given acts depending on what motivated them, even though the results of the acts are the same. The perceived value of or satisfaction produced by acts with good and bad motivation, therefore, may be different. In some cases, the difference between the different kinds of acts may be great enough in terms of satisfaction actually to change whether or not the acts are valued positively, even though the results of the two acts are the same. In any event, most people have a preference for good motivations qua good motivations.

An intuitive feel for what is at stake here is provided by the dictum of Oliver Wendell Holmes that "even a dog distinguishes between being stumbled over and being kicked."[8] Another example is provided by the importance of the motive of sincerity. If a person does us a favor because he likes us, we react differently than if the person does us the same favor with the hope that we will get him something he wants. Many people, for instance, care about the motivations of politicians. If a politician's act is perceived as being motivated simply by a desire to "take credit" for the results, many people react cynically; one of the reasons for the low reputation of politicians is that they are seen as lacking sincere motivations for their acts, even when the acts produce good results.

Take also the situation of the employer who improves working conditions for his employees in response to market conditions—improving conditions is cheaper than paying the wage premium necessary to attract people to work under the poorer conditions, or making the changes can pay for itself in improved productivity. To an economist, this is a superb example of how the market works (without laws or regulations, it is often noted). Yet, if workers perceive that employers are improving conditions in order to make money, their satisfaction with the changes may well be less than if the employer made the change for another reason—say, out of concern for the workers or because of a law the workers got the government to pass—even though the results, in terms of working conditions, are the same in the two instances. (In turn, different levels of satisfaction may produce different productivity consequences in the two situations, even though the same changes were made. But that is a separate story.) By this view, pollution reductions achieved only because they were cheaper than paying a charge may not be valued as highly as equivalent reductions motivated by lawabidingness or concern for others.

These psychological feelings, in the view of the author of one textbook on criminal law, are at the root of the doctrine of criminal intent.[9]

> *Deeply ingrained in human nature is the tendency to distinguish intended results from accidental happenings. . . . (O)ne who has been painfully injured by another's act will not have the same personal resentment if it was obviously an accidental injury as he will if the harm was inflicted upon him intentionally.*

Note that we do not inquire here into why good motivations should make people on the receiving end for them feel good. Perhaps such a feeling arises due to a past association of good motivations with good results. Perhaps it arises because good motivations give an evidence of others' interest in our welfare that we appreciate. I suspect that many economists might regard the value ascribed good motives as "irrational." Why should a worker care, I imagine many economists would ask, what the reasons were that his boss improved working conditions? Certainly, standard economics textbooks write frequently about preferences for oranges or Caribbean vacations, but seldom about preferences for good motivations. To the extent economists begin questioning the importance many people attribute to positive feelings associated with good motivations, they depart from their own self-image as scholars who take preferences as givens, not entering the fray of battling for what preferences people ought to have. They are abandoning their nonjudgmentalism about people's preferences. Indeed, I believe that efforts by economists to emphasize the value of self-interest in social life definitely involve attempts to influence people's preferences in the direction of valuing certain motivations (namely, self-interest) more highly than might otherwise have been the case.

One way to conceptualize the preference for good motivations into the model of caring only about results is to see what is occurring in cases of acts with good and bad motivations as two different behaviors. Stumbling over a dog is not the same behavior as kicking it; insincere favors, political activity, or employer efforts to improve working conditions are not the same as sincere versions of the same actions. That the results are different would, then, not be surprising; the behaviors are different.

Like the suggestion that bad motivations encourage bad results over a wider universe of results, the view that behavior with bad motivation is different behavior and thus can bring about worse results is an attempt to recognize the importance of motives, although within a "nothing matters but results" framework. The advance that this expanded view makes is that it recognizes a psychological attitude, and not just a physical state of the world, as a part both of the behavior and of the results it produces.

But it is possible to take the argument even further. Doing so involves what philosophers would regard as the intrinsic value of good motives and/or the intrinsic moral rightness of acts with good motivations. The suggestion has been made that a worker may not feel as good about a given improvement in working conditions if he believes it was just done to save the employer money. But we may also argue that good motives are *intrinsically* good, over and above the satisfaction they may produce, while bad motives are intrinsically bad, over and above any bad results they produce. By things that are "intrinsically" good, philosophers mean things that are valued for themselves. Things such as food or shelter are not intrinsically good, but are only goods instrumental to production of the intrinsic good of satisfaction. Almost every philosopher, except some ascetics, agrees that satisfaction is an intrinsic good. The debate is whether it is the *only* intrinsic good—that is, whether one can attribute value to any other things, even if they don't produce satisfaction.[10] This was Kant's position when he wrote of "the absolute value of good will," which, even if it "should be wholly lacking in power to accomplish its purpose" would still "sparkle like a jewel in its own right, as something that had its full worth in itself."[11] A person who believes that good motivation is intrinsically good would argue that it was better for an employer to act sincerely towards employees even if it didn't make the employees more satisfied than they otherwise would have been and even if nobody else, who might feel differently about the well-motivated and badly motivated acts, knew about it.

When economists use the word "utility," the question of whether satisfaction is the only thing of value becomes somewhat obscured, since utility-producing things are variously defined both as things that are valued and things that produce satisfaction. But there is a genuine debate among philosophers, frequently involving such possible intrinsic goods as knowledge (Is there intrinsic good to knowing something, even if that knowledge makes us unhappy?) or beauty (Is there intrinsic good to a beautiful thing, even if nobody observes it?). Or, to take an example more related to public policy issues, is our only objection to giving slum dwellers economic incentives to prepare garbage neatly for collection the one that doing so would produce a bad universe of results? Or do we value an attitude of personal responsibility in people just for itself? Furthermore, without wishing to get into a technical discussion of ethical theory, we may note that one might argue that well-motivated acts tend to be morally right even over and above the good they produce (whether in terms of satisfaction or in terms of any other intrinsic good) because they show respect for the dignity of persons. This is the position Charles Fried takes in arguing for the importance of good intention. If one regards good motivation as an intrinsic good beyond any satisfaction well-motivated acts produce, and/or if one regards well-motivated acts as tending to be morally right beyond any good they produce, one moves towards a view of the importance of good motivations that extends beyond even the broadest of "what matters is results" approaches. One also moves furthest away from the conceptual world of the microeconomic paradigm—a reason why some of the above discussion is likely to appear somewhat strange to many whose main grounding is in the paradigm. (It is, by contrast, basic dime store ethical theory.)

Up to this point, the expression "good motivation" has been used without formally presenting an argument about why certain motivations might be, in fact, good. As argued previously, this should in a sense not be necessary for economists; the simple existence of such preferences should be accepted as a *datum*. Nevertheless, I wish to make an argument in the remainder of this section for why it is justified to value altruistic motivations, contrasting this with the eagerness of advocates of economic incentives to harness self-interest. Altruism will be regarded as a specific example of a good motivation.

The Value of Altruism vs. Self-Interest

Certainly, few reasonable people would deny the important role self-interest plays in human behavior. Furthermore, most people would probably agree that there are important areas of life where self-interest has a benign or salutary effect. Two questions remain, however. First, does altruism have value as well? Second, if it does, should we be careful about changes in the boundaries of the areas where we encourage altruism and areas where we are indifferent to whether it exists or not?

Altruistic behavior is that motivated out of concern for others. It is possible to claim that such behavior never occurs—that all behavior apparently undertaken out of such concern in fact has some self-interested cause such as the desire to feel good by helping others.[12] One version of this claim is that seeming examples of altruism in reality often involve situations where individuals expect to get something in return from those towards whom they behave in an altruistic way. One example sometimes adduced involves situations where if everyone behaved self-interestedly, the consequences would be bad (such as in taking a short cut by walking over a flower bed in a park). Others involve situations where people behave in a certain way when they have benefitted or might in the future benefit from similar altruistic behavior from others (such as in donating blood). But such behaviors are not trades in the sense that avoiding the bad consequences or gaining the benefits is not *contingent on* the altruistic behavior. (Someone who gives blood because he was once aided by a blood donor in the past would have gotten the blood in the past whether or not he gives it now.)

The claim that all seeming examples of altruism are really self-interested often reduces into a definitional statement that would be impossible to refute by any example. There meanwhile remains a distinction that most people feel between acts motivated by something we may call "X" and others motivated by something different we may call "Y." It is possible to state in everyday language that "I would have preferred to act selfishly, but I chose to act altruistically because it was the right thing to do." If people did not feel a distinction between these two motivations for behavior, such a sentence would not make sense. If unhappy with the designations of "self-interest" for "X" and "altruism" for "Y," the reader may invent his own terms.

Like other good motives, altruistic motives may have value both for their results and for their intrinsic qualities. The results of a world without altruism would be grim. Altruistic behavior is central to the functioning of society as we know it. As Edmund Phelps has noted, "More than one half of the American population depend for their security and material satisfactions not upon the sale of their services, but rather on their relationships with others."[13] For many of these people—children, housewives, the elderly—the existence of altruistic behavior may make the difference between survival and nonsurvival.

Altruism is potentially important whenever one person's self-interested behavior has external effects. As noted earlier, in cases where behavior has external effects, not dealt with through property or liability rules, self-interest does not automatically maximize social welfare even in a market regime. When such situations exist, altruism is a way of bringing about a situation where some injuries to others do not occur. If it can be summoned forth, altruistic behavior is more efficient than self-interested behavior any time that the transaction costs of detecting harmful self-interested behavior or of contracting between the parties so that one party agrees to avoid injuring the other are greater than the benefits to the victim from undertaking the detection, but less than the cost to the perpetrator from behaving in a non-self-interested way. A butcher declines to short-weight the meat he sells a customer, though the expected cost of detection by the customer would be greater than the customer's expected loss. A person finds a wallet containing $50 on the street and calls up the owner, even though the cost of detecting the person who found the wallet would be many times that amount. A passer-by throws a drowning man a buoy, without bothering to enter into negotiations with the man about how much he would be willing to pay to be rescued.

The point is that such situations occur repeatedly in the widest range of social interactions. In such cases, it is possible to conceptualize the situation in terms of ill-defined property rights producing overproduction of an injury. One might say, for instance, that there is excessive production of meanness because its victims have no property right in consideration—just as economists do when they conceptualize pollution. But it would be incredibly difficult and costly to set up a system where economic incentives made it in people's self-interest to behave appropriately in all the myriad ways when self-interest would not make us do so otherwise. Altruism is a cheaper way. It produces better results. Altruism is not only cheaper in terms of money spent. The image of a society with the degree of controls necessary to channel the exercise of self-interest into appropriate paths whenever such behavior led to bad results is a terrible one, not only for the surveillance and interference with people's lives it implies, but for the sweeping aside of personal responsibility it represents. This last, I think, is an important point. "Social engineering" of unparalleled scope would be the result of a world where we attempted to translate consistently the economist's dictum that inappropriate behavior be made appropriate behavior by relying on economic incentives.

Altruistic motives may also be a source of satisfaction in themselves. If someone returns a lost wallet with $50 in it, most people would value the act itself, above and beyond the return of their $50; the altruistic act itself is a source of satisfaction. By contrast, a voluntary exchange of goods between two people where each perceives the other as self-interested may produce smaller gains from trade than the exact same exchange of goods where the parties are altruistic; the idea that one is being "used" by others for their own gain, even if we gain as well, may frequently be a source of dissatisfaction.

Finally, altruistic behavior may be morally right even in circumstances when it would not be efficient; that is, where its
benefits did not outweigh its costs. This would be in cases where
we regarded the behavior as fulfilling duties, say, to be honest
or to respect the value of life. Landes and Posner note the value
of altruism in the case of a drowning man in terms of the transaction costs of reaching an agreement between the potential rescuer and the drowning man.[14] Surely, they note, such an agreement would be made were it possible—the cost to the rescuer
is minimal, and the benefit to the drowning man is great. They
would thus, if they were able to contract, be able to agree on a
price for the rescue. But this is a contingent set of facts. Imagine
an alternate fact situation. The drowning man is penniless and too
old to work, while the potential rescuer, a wealthy man, is afraid
that stopping to rescue the victim will cause him to miss the start
of a football game he has been anticipating for weeks. Under such
circumstances, it is plausible that no agreement would have been
reached. Should one be indifferent to the presence or absence
of altruism under such circumstances? Most people, I think, would
regard an altruistic act under these circumstances as being morally
right whether or not an agreement would have been reached. It
is not simply a question of altruism being more efficient given
high transaction costs.

Because altruistic behavior frequently brings about better results than self-interested behavior, because altruistic behavior is
a source of satisfaction in itself, and because altruistic behavior
may in many circumstances be morally right, I believe most people
want to see a place for altruistic behavior among people in our
society—or, indeed, wish to see more altruism than currently
exists. Our society now has a certain mix of the use of self-interest
and the use of altruism to achieve desired social behavior. Neither
is relied on exclusively. A society where frequent use of altruism
was abandoned as a way of achieving desirable social behavior and
a decision made always to accept self-interest and merely try to
"harness" it through economic incentives would be a radically
different society from our own. *Any decision about changing the
mix of methods used for bringing about desirable social behavior
is thus a decision that influences what kind of society we live in.*

The political sphere of life—the sphere where people decide
on what actions to undertake collectively—is, because it involves
others and not just one's self, a sphere where concern for others

may play an especially important role. This does not mean, obviously, that when most people act politically they always act out of concern for others. Self-interest, of course, plays a crucial role in political as in private life. But self-interest does not have the legitimacy in political life that it has in market relations. The most narrow of special interest groups feels the need to present its arguments in public-spirited terms. To give self-interest a greater role in the political sphere—in decisions about what actions we undertake collectively—would have a special significance because it would involve abandoning the importance attached to concern for others in a sphere of life, the public sphere, where it traditionally has had pride of place. It is difficult to believe that such an abandonment would not signal a lower weight society attributes to such values and hence discourage development of preferences that give concern for others a strong weight. This signal might be especially unfortunate not so much with regard to preferences of polluters—for whom, it might be argued, it is utopian to expect that they will reduce pollution out of altruism in any event—as for the preferences of citizens in general.

Two objections to the view presented here should be discussed. The first would accept the value of altruism, but argue that since it is in short supply, it should be husbanded for where there is no other alternative.[15] Surely this view is correct to the extent that it is unrealistic to believe that altruism can regulate all human interactions—and perhaps undesirable as well, given the costs of gathering information on the desires of others. Yet the view that altruism, or any other value, is in fixed supply surely ignores the influence of the world around us on the development of our preferences. It seems more plausible to believe that the more concern for others we see around us, and the more we see concern for others honored, the more likely we are to give such values a strong weight.

A second objection might be that the difference between the motivations that economic incentives and the current regulatory system involve is not that great. While an economic incentive approach to environmental regulation would openly enshrine self-interested motivations in this area of public policy, it would of course be incorrect to claim that the current alternative regime of legal commands enshrines altruistic motivations. Much obedience to legal commands, obviously, comes from a self-interested desire to avoid being punished. One problem with this objection is that it is the advocates of "the public use of private interests" who originated the dichotomy between a regime of legal commands and one of economic incentives that appeal to self-interest. Furthermore, it is true that, while economic incentives require only self-interested motives, compliance with legal demands tends, among most citizens, to be predicated on a wider range of motivations. Fear of punishment may certainly be present. But obedience to laws gains additional support from the view that the legal system embodies rules that are a statement of people's mutual concern for each other's interests. And the fear of social stigma, as opposed to economic or physical punishment, that is also often part of obedience to laws reflects our situation as social beings interrelated each of us to others. Reminders of our dependence on each other may in turn encourage altruism or other positively valued feelings and morally right behaviors. An attitude of law-abidingness, indeed, may be seen as a sort of automatic altruism for a person's everyday life.

In conclusion, then, there are reasons to be critical of social decisions that increase the role of self-interest as a motivation. This is a reason to be concerned with the use of economic incentives in environmental policy.

Wishing to Stigmatize Polluting Behavior

One of the most frequently expressed concerns of critics about the use of economic incentives in environmental policy is that they would grant an unacceptable "license to pollute"; to use economic incentives would express society's indifference about whether or not polluting behavior occurred as long as the charge was paid. Economists who discuss objections made to charges have had trouble suppressing contempt for the "license to pollute" contention, which they interpret merely as an argument that, faced with a pollution charge, polluters simply will pay the charge and continue to pollute as much as before. Such an argument, in their view, demonstrates ignorance of the insight, fundamental to economics, that if something becomes more expensive to do, less of it will be done. To the extent that they are willing to accept the "license to pollute" vocabulary at all, economists would give the counterargument that license fees are low charges, too low to diminish by much the behavior in question. If the pollution charge is set at an appropriately high level, it is continued, it certainly will decrease polluting behavior.

The thinly disguised contempt that most economists feel about the "license to pollute" worry displays, I believe, a failure to appreciate the importance many people attribute to feelings inside people's heads. And the counterarguments fail to address the worry at that level. Licenses are normally given out to authorize behavior toward which society takes a positive, or at least neutral, attitude. Practicing medicine, driving a car, or getting married are not regarded as undesirable activities. A license is needed to perform these behaviors in order to assure that those performing them are competent enough to meet certain legal requirements. In other cases, as with a license to own a dog, the behavior is also approved, and the main purpose of the license requirement is to raise revenue. What many of those who worry about charges being a "license to pollute" react against is the implied authorization of polluting behavior that charges represent. The fear is that by replacing standards, which are social statements of acceptable and unacceptable behavior, with charges, society would be saying, in effect, that "it's OK to pollute as long as you pay a fee." There is reason to be concerned about the use of economic incentives in environmental policy because they fail to make a social statement stigmatizing polluting behavior.

Certainly, the legal system does reflect the intuitive distinction most people make between some harms that cause economic damage—and are thus unacceptable only to the extent that the victim is not compensated for the costs incurred—and others that involve something else as well, because they violate what people see as moral rules. These harms are thus especially stigmatized by the legal system. There existed, for example, a distinction in the early common law between a *malum in se* and a *malum prohibitum*. The initial distinction was between offenses (such as murder or rape) that were wrong "quite apart from the fact that they are offences in English law" and those (such as parking in an illegal area) that are "the creature of the legislative, which has made, unmade, and altered such offences as it has thought fit."[16] The King "could license the subject to commit a *malum prohibitum*, . . . [but] he could not licence the subject to commit an offence *malum in se*."[17]

> *In Blackstone's view, the fine attached to a* malum prohibitum *did
> not . . . place upon the individual any duty of compliance. He
> could obey the law and avoid the penalty or violate the law and
> pay the fine. Which election he made was a matter of indifference
> except to himself.*

Compare this with the attitude towards, say, robbery and rape.
What is the role of penalties in regard to such behaviors? When
we criminalize bank robbery and set the penalty as five years in
prison, we are not saying it is all right to rob a bank if you are
"willing to pay" the penalty for it. We are saying that people
shouldn't rob banks and are setting a penalty of five years in prison
as a signal of our disapproval. We do not accept a utilitarian
argument that a desperately poor man be able to break the law
prohibiting bank robberies even if it can be demonstrated that
the money would mean more to him than to the depositors.

One may note in this context the writings of some economists
regarding the "optimal" amount of fraud and the "optimal" level
of the enforcement of laws.[18] Most people would react, probably
with some vehemence, that the "optimal" level of fraud is zero
and the "optimal" level of enforcement is complete. When economists suggest this is not the case, the point they are making is
basically the simple one that at some point the fraud or crime
detected by marginal efforts to prevent them do not justify additional marginal resources devoted to prevention. If explained
this way, most people would probably agree. However, they would
likely add something like, "But 'optimal' is normally a moral term,
something that expresses a positive attitude towards a situation.
You are using the word in a different way." And thus the heart
of the disagreement is reached: to most people, a moral condemnation of fraud or other crime is important, and the statement
that some level other than zero is optimal counteracts that necessary moral condemnation.

Those who believe that polluting the environment is criminal
feel similarly. It is not, they might argue, "all right" to pollute
the environment just because one is willing to pay the charge.
And the firm with high abatement costs (the analogy to the desperately poor man) should not be exempted from its duty on
utilitarian grounds.

There are three grounds for wishing to see a social decision
process stigmatize polluting behavior by declaring it illegal not
to do "the best one can" to end it. First, such stigmatization

provides an occasion for a social statement expressing a judgment condemning such behavior, a judgment that pleases environmentalists. Second, such stigmatization encourages development of preferences that attach a strong weight to high environmental quality. Third, such stigmatization encourages compliance by polluters with environmental demands.

Society's Judgments

The first reason why environmentalists would wish to avoid an environmental policy that did not include as part of it a social statement of condemnation is that they wish society to express a judgment stigmatizing such behavior. In so wishing they are, I think, expressing a judgmentalism that is very common among people and applying it to something that they feel strongly about, namely, polluting behavior. It is a rare human being who does not adopt visceral judgmental attitudes—praise or condemnation—towards many behaviors. We like, or don't like, people who wear flashy clothes. We like, or don't like, people who are diffident. The tendency to be judgmental probably arises from the basic cognitive need to categorize the things around us—for without categorizations, we could make no sense of the myriad of sensory stimuli that bombard us. This visceral tendency to be judgmental flies in the face of the nonjudgmentalism the economic paradigm endorses and the concomitant inability to appreciate demands that reflect judgmental attitudes towards, say, polluting behavior. At the same time, a liberal society encourages tolerance. There is thus also a side of most people that resents the "busybody" and endorses the notion of "live and let live." There is an internal war in the psyches of most people between their judgmental side and their tolerant side.

One of the grounds for adopting condemnatory attitudes towards the behavior of others may be the costs such behavior imposes on third parties. It is this grounds for condemnation that appears to be dealt with if one requires payment equivalent to the harm. But this is not the only grounds for such condemnatory attitudes. If the behavior has costs in terms of things not traded in markets, one may believe that such costs cannot, or one may not want them to be (for reasons to be discussed below), fully expressed in monetary terms. If this is the case, paying the monetary costs of the behavior does not fully compensate for the behavior. Violent behaviors, such as rape or robbery, fall into this category. So do lies or other behaviors that violate moral rules. The scores of everyday interactions—politeness or impoliteness, consideration or inconsideration, and so forth—that can obviously never be integrated into a system of charging for external effects of behavior belong here as well. Polluting behavior that involves harms to non-priced things may be placed in the same category. But even if a behavior could be fully compensated for by paying a certain amount of money, many might still feel that this behavior should be condemned. Such a feeling may be a remnant of the long period when people were able wantonly to impose the costs of behavior on others without compensating them. It may reflect condemnation of those who still "get away" without paying the compensation. It may reflect a realization that the transaction costs of obtaining the compensation still often fall on the victims or on society. Finally, one may condemn certain behaviors, beyond their effects on others, simply because one doesn't like them. There is, of course, no place for such condemnation in economics, but certainly such condemnation is a common feature of human life. Few people would be indifferent in their judgments of a person, say, who chose to spend his evenings alone at home locked in a cage staring at a blue light, or of a person who chooses to keep the inside of his home looking like a pigsty. Similarly, and sep-arately, one may be concerned about the level of blue light staring as opposed to, say, book reading, in the society where one lives. It is possible to conceptualize these concerns as unpaid-for external costs that others impose (you impose an external cost on me if you stare at a blue light, because it gives me dissatisfaction), and thus reintegrate the concern into the standard microeconomic model of justified concern in cases of external costs. But it should be noted that the external cost occurs only because of the initial judgmentalism about an individual's personal behavior.

And, just as good motives might be considered desirable both to encourage good behavior and as good in themselves (or right in themselves), the same may be said for the role of condemnatory judgments of the improper behavior of others. Stigmatization, as will be noted below, encourages good behavior. And stigmatization may be good intrinsically (or right in itself), because it can be seen as just that good behavior be praised and bad behavior condemned.

Developing Proenvironment Preferences

The second reason for wishing to see a stigmatization of polluting behavior take place is to give citizens a signal encouraging them to develop preferences that give the environment a strong weight. There is an unresolved debate over to what extent laws change people's values: did civil rights laws tend to erode racial prejudice in the South, for instance? But environmentalists are deeply involved in the business of battling for the minds of citizens, trying to encourage people to develop preferences that give achievement of good environmental quality a high weight. Statements by environmentalists frequently emphasize the importance of developing an "environmental ethic," which is the way they express the importance of what they would call the "consciousness-raising" process they are involved in. Hence they can be expected to welcome a social statement condemning polluters as something that will help them in their battle. And, since decisions about what levels of environmental cleanup to seek are social decisions, environmentalists have obvious reason to be concerned about what preferences other citizens have, because these preferences will influence the outcome of the social decisions. Whether or not polluting behavior is stigmatized will tend, therefore, to influence what level of cleanup demands society ends up making. The question of means chosen to achieve a given level of cleanup and the level of cleanup selected are not independent, as economic incentive advocates suggest. The "license to pollute" that an economic incentives policy implies may influence citizen preferences in a direction that gives achievement of a clean environment less weight—and hence lower the level of cleanup that society finally requires. Yet this is a dynamic for which one can have little appreciation if one simply takes preferences as givens.

An important distinction should, however, be noted. It is one thing to recognize that advocates of various values seek to get others to value highly the things they value highly themselves. It is another thing to suggest that the power of the state be used to favor one set of values over another. It is a strongly embedded aspect of our traditions of liberal tolerance that we accept the legitimacy of people with different values jostling for the support of citizens, while government remains neutral among the contenders. By this view, it may be argued that it is an illegitimate grounds for favoring standards over economic incentives in environmental policy to state that the former policy expresses an attitude of social stigmatization towards polluting behavior. Such stigmatization, in this view, is not a legitimate role for government to play.

The problem with this argument is that any time government adopts laws in an area, these laws may well turn out to influence the values citizens hold. This is the case even for the most minimal laws that libertarians would favor, such as laws against murder. That murder is illegal almost certainly plays a role in affecting people's attitude towards it, for making murder criminal says more about society's attitude towards it than that society will punish those who murder. It also stigmatizes murder and encourages the development of preferences that give respect for life a strong weight. In any society with laws, complete government neutrality about values cannot exist. Once government adopts a policy for dealing with environmental pollution—a policy decision that advocates of charges question no more than advocates of standards— the choice between standards and charges is not a choice between government partiality and government neutrality. *Either* policy will reflect a different social statement about polluting behavior and will tend thus to influence people's preferences.

In his work on liability rules in the legal system, Mark Kelman comes to a similar conclusion from somewhat different starting points. [19] He begins by noting that there exists evidence that people demand to be paid more to give up a thing they currently enjoy than they would be willing to pay to gain the same thing if they don't already have it. What this means is that the strength of our preference for some thing x will tend to *vary* depending on whether we are initially assigned a right to x or whether we are not and must pay for it instead. He continues by pointing out that the assignment of rights and liabilities by the legal system either puts people in a position where they have the right to something (say, quiet surroundings) and need to be paid in order to give it up, or in a position where they have no right to the thing and must pay others to obtain it. Therefore, Kelman concludes, assignment of liability rules affects the strength of preferences. Kelman continues by noting that all writers on liability rules concede that often transactions costs are too great to make a situation without liability rules, where rights are simply negotiated among the parties, an optimal one—and that therefore an important task of the legal system is to assign rights and liabilities. If government inevitably is involved in the business of establishing liability rules, and if establishment of liability rules inevitably influences preferences, then government actions inevitably influence preferences.

Several points should be noted in relation to all this. First, to influence is not the same as to command. That a policy stigmatizes polluting behavior does not mean that it commands that citizens adhere to preferences that give environmental quality a strong weight or prohibits dissemination of views that seek to persuade citizens that environmental policy is not important at all. Second, one may draw a line that accepts the value of tolerance and government neutrality among competing ideas by stating that government ought not decide to restrict individual liberty to behave as one wishes in a given area *in order to* influence citizen preferences. In other words, the decision to regulate or limit behavior in a certain area should stand on its own, without reference to the implications of such restrictions on citizen preferences. Thus, for example, decisions to limit an individual's freedom to kill others—or to pollute the environment—must be made on their own merits. This test would exclude, for example, policies whose only purpose was to influence preferences. But once it is decided, *on other grounds*, to regulate or limit behavior in a certain area, the (necessary) implications of alternative policies for citizen preferences should be faced honestly. When society has decided to adopt a policy forbidding murder, little criticism is expressed over the fact that this social decision also has the effect of stigmatizing murder. The suggestion that it is *possible* for government always to remain neutral hinders a facing up to issues that need to be faced.

A final point may be made regarding governmental intervention in the process of preference formation. One may worry that government indifference towards people's ideas might extinguish the value people attach to having any ideas at all. It was noted in the beginning of this discussion that, at the individual level, most people have both judgmental and tolerant sides. At the societal level, one line of criticism of the liberal commitment to tolerance has been that it reflects an indifference towards the value of ideas. One reason for being tolerant of diverse views, it is sometimes suggested, might be that one does not really care very much one way or the other about what views people have. Critics who take this view sometimes suggest that the historical connection between the growth of capitalist market economies and of pluralistic tolerance results partly from the spread of the view that one ought to forget about abstract ideas—such as the various religious beliefs about which people frequently battled—and "settle down" to making money.[20]

A similar problem may grow out of the explicit decision in microeconomic theory to take preferences as givens and not to discuss them further. The problem is that the salience of various values that compete for our favor often depends significantly on how often and how insistently we are exposed to them.[21] It is sometimes suggested, for instance, that the constant emphasis in most writings by economists on efficiency compared with equity (an emphasis economists justify by pointing to their ability to draw conclusions about the former but not the latter) in fact influences those exposed to it towards caring about efficiency and not equity. Something similar may occur with regard to the refusal to say anything about preferences. Lack of attention to preferences can produce in those exposed to microeconomics a lack of concern about the importance of preferences.

My own view, which I will not defend here, is that it is right for government to be impartial when such impartiality is possible. At the same time, the existence of instances, such as those described above, where such impartiality is simply impossible allows one, so to speak, to have one's cake and eat it too. Impartiality can be maintained where it is a feasible alternative, and influence over preferences in situations where such cannot be avoided provides an occasion for society to signal that ideas are indeed valued.

The third reason for wanting to stigmatize polluting behavior is the effect such stigmatization might have on the behavior of pollutors. Decisions to seek to reduce levels of pollution are not self-enforcing. (The view of some advocates of charges that dealing with pollution through the tax system rather than a regulatory system makes environmental policy self-enforcing is certainly a wild exaggeration.) Stigmatization of polluting behavior will tend to increase compliance with social measures to reduce pollution. Stigmatization may also act to make polluters realize that their behavior shows insufficient concern for others, thus changing their attitudes and, perhaps, their resistance to environmental laws. This may occur, as noted briefly earlier, because of the connection of the success of stigmatization with the existence of a sense of social interdependence. Feeling the sting of the condemnation of one's fellows can make one realize that one's fellows are indeed important factors in one's life. To give up the opportunity to stigmatize polluting behavior will thus tend to increase the amount of pollution generated or, alternatively, to increase the other resources society must put into compliance. Failure to stigmatize may also work against development of altruistic motivations that have worth themselves and also may influence positions polluters take in political debates on environmental legislation.

A counterargument to the entire line of reasoning above could be made to the effect that environmental regulation using standards no more forbids polluting behavior than does economic incentives, since such regulation forbids pollution only insofar as the standard is violated. Below that, polluting behavior is permitted. This is in contrast to, say, murder, of which even one is prohibited. One might argue that under a standards regime, "It's OK to pollute as long as it is below the standard." (Indeed, one advantage an environmentalist might see in charges—and that a businessman might worry about—is that pollution even below the level of the standard would be discouraged.)

There is, nonetheless, a difference. What environmentalists wish to ask polluters to do is "the best they can" to reduce pollution, even if "the best they can" doesn't mean they eliminate pollution entirely. "Can," in everyday language, implies some limits of physical capability—a technology that doesn't exist or costs that would drive a company out of business. A response that falls much short of that—whatever else its virtues might possibly be—does not meet the everyday language meaning of "do the best you can." It might be *efficient* for a high abatement-cost polluter hardly to reduce pollution at all if there are many low abatement-cost polluters around. For the high-cost abater to do little or nothing, however, when doing something would not be technologically complex and not threaten the viability of the firm, would not be, whatever else it was, to "do the best one can." Thus, the difference in terms of stigmatization of polluting behavior between standards and charges does exist, if the former requires, as environmentalists wish them to, that polluters do the best they can.[22]

In conclusion, then, there are reasons to seek social decisions that stigmatize polluting behavior. This is a reason to be concerned with the use of economic incentives in environmental policy.

Reasons for Opposing Establishment of Markets or Prices for Things Not Previously Traded in Markets or Priced

"The market" is a method that uses prices to steer production and allocation of things.* It involves permitting sellers to put things up for sale to buyers who might be interested in purchasing them. To the things put up for sale, a price comes to be attached (usually a money price). Producers of a thing base production decisions on price signals.

Broadly speaking, there are three ways valued things are produced or allocated in our society. One is the market. The second is private nonmarket methods. The third is government. In our society, many things are habitually bought and sold on markets. But many are not. Human beings are not bought and sold, and no market price is attached to them. The same goes for many behaviors one person may display towards another—friendship, approval, love, hatred. And many entitlements established by law—the right to vote, freedom of speech, the right to "equal employment opportunity" established for blacks and women in civil rights legislation, or the right to a "safe and healthy workplace" established for workers by the Occupational Safety and Health Act—are not habitually bought and sold either, and no price is attached to them. And this goes as well for many elements of our natural surroundings. Air is not habitually bought and sold in the market; water is to a limited degree, mainly when it is removed from its natural surroundings. Forests, mountains, beaches, and wetlands are kept at least to an extent off the market. (In some other countries, they are kept off the market completely.)

The efficiency advantages of steering production and allocation through prices were discussed earlier and need not be repeated. As noted then, the efficiency argument for using prices to steer levels and allocation of the production of pollution (and thereby environmental quality) are simply adaptations of the general argument to a specific instance. In economic analysis, problems of market failure (such as monopoly or high information or transaction

---

* I shall use the inelegant word "things" as a general expression to cover material objects, behaviors, and entitlements to behave in certain ways without interference, or to demand certain behaviors of others. If I wish to speak of material objects specifically, I shall use the word "goods."

costs) and of equity are frequently adduced as reasons against allowing markets to function without further intervention. There exist also, however, different kinds of objections to using markets and prices as a method to steer production and allocation. These objections are less familiar to economists, but all the more familiar to most other people. Markets are an institution where humans interact, and hence there is much more to them than their efficiency-related properties. The nature of the human interactions in market exchange is thus a candidate for examination. An unease exists among most people about the consequences of having all human interactions occur as market exchanges and attaching a money price to all valued things. The unease translates into opposition against having some things bought and sold on markets at all, a concern that the market sector not be permitted to encroach further into the private nonmarket or the government sectors. One may oppose use of economic incentives in environmental policy out of the desire not to have more nonmarketed things brought into the realm of the market.

Anxiety about the spread of the market has been one of the main currents in the writings of sociologists about market-based societies ever since Ferdinand Toennies wrote of the distinction between *Gemeinschaft* and *Gesellschaft* and Max Weber worried about the consequences of the "demystification" of all aspects of life under the influence of the spread of rational calculation. The unease is by no means confined to scholars who write about society. It is given expression—"above all," one is tempted to add—in the metaphors of everyday language and the images of everyday life. We attack people for "prostituting" themselves by selling some things for money. The expression "businesslike" may be fine to describe the relationship among businessmen, but hardly between parents and children or between friends. We tell ourselves that love of money is the root of all evil. Such unease is a common theme in literature as well, even dominating one of the important literary movements (Romanticism) in the period around the beginnings of industrialization. Blake decried the "dark satanic mills," and Ruskin praised the Gothic architecture of the Middle Ages as a representation of a better view of relationships among people. Dickens wrote of Ebenezer Scrooge in *A Christmas Carol*, "squeezing, wrenching, grasping, scraping, clutching,"[23] and of Gradgrind in *Hard Times*, "a man of facts and calculations" who believed that "everything was to be paid for" and "nobody was

ever on any account to give anybody anything, or render anybody
help without purchase"—and who ended up destroying the lives
of the people around him.[24] The novels of Flaubert presented
fathers who sold their children for money and businessmen who
rushed away from the funeral of a partner, glad that it didn't take
too long.

That themes so common, not only in the writings of scholars
in other fields but in literature and in everyday life as well, are
largely ignored by economists when they praise markets is striking.
One reason for this may be that the unease tends to be presented
in intuitive form. People, including scholars and novelists, aren't
forced to analyze their intuitions unless faced with challenges to
them. Few people ever get challenged unless they have dealt on
a sustained basis with economists.

Like all efforts to analyze intuitions, the effort to analyze the
sources of unease with markets turns out to be a difficult one, not
in least because it frequently develops that people have several
concepts in minds when they express an intuition. (And different
people may well have different concepts in mind, all the while
expressing the same intuition.)

The essential argument is that the very use of the market for
steering production and allocation of a thing imposes costs. This
occurs in two ways.

First, using the market may decrease production of certain
behaviors that induce valued feelings. It need hardly be argued
that there exist many feelings to which most people ascribe a
positive value. One feeling, pleasure (broadly defined), is recognized as an important intrinsic good by almost everyone who
has thought about the subject, and the *only* intrinsic good by
some. Other positive feelings—such as exhiliration, gaiety, a sense
of security, pride in accomplishment, the feeling of love, the
feeling of being loved, and so forth—may then be valued, just as
other things (such as television sets or yacht trips) are valued, as
means to achieving greater feelings of pleasure. Other feelings
have a negative value for most people. One could cite loneliness,
sadness, or the feeling of being disliked, but, again, the list could
be extended considerably. If an action produces decreased production of valued feelings or increased production of disvalued
feelings, it therefore imposes costs.

Second, exchanging something on the market and placing a
price on it may itself reduce the perceived value of the thing.

What is taking place is not a cost in terms of decreased production of positively valued feelings due to market exchange in good x. It is, instead, a direct decrease in the perceived value of x itself. This is not a mere shift in tastes as would occur if people value hula-hoops one year and skateboards another. The strength of the preference for x has decreased without the strength of preferences for any other things increasing.

These two processes may be dubbed the "feeling-falloff effect" and the "downvaluation effect." Together they constitute psychological costs of using the market—psychological in the one instance because the feelings whose production goes down are in the mind and in the other instance because the value we choose to ascribe a thing comes, in the final instance, from the mind.[25]

The Feeling-Falloff Effect

I will first discuss the feeling-falloff effect. A discussion of feeling-inducing behaviors encouraged or discouraged by use of the market should begin with the observation that the value feelings have implies inevitable limitations of the role of markets. It is impossible directly to buy or sell a feeling. The best I can do is to buy or sell a good or behavior that tends to induce a certain feeling in myself or in others. And, insofar as such behaviors are concerned, there are major limits to the ability to induce their increased production or determine their allocation through the market as well. I may agree to praise a person in exchange for cash, but the feeling induced by being the object of praise may come only for a behavior that may be dubbed "praise not bought for cash." Praise not bought for cash can by definition not be bought for cash, and this places an inexorable limit on the ability to increase its production using the market.

I will discuss several feeling-inducing behaviors whose production is either encouraged or discouraged by the specific form of human interaction called market exchange. Spontaneity and altruism are among behaviors that induce positively valued feelings, but which market exchange punishes. Calculation and self-interestedness are among the behaviors market exchange favors, but these behaviors either fail to induce positively valued feelings or, in some instances, actually induce negatively valued feelings. The behaviors that market exchange requires if its efficiency benefits are to be fully realized include impersonal and competitive relationships among people, but these behaviors too fail to induce positively valued feelings, or in some instances induce negatively valued feelings. Personalized and cooperative relationships are behaviors that become more scarce. (Nothing to be stated here, it should be noted, argues that the behaviors that produce negative feelings exist *only* in market relationships, simply that there are aspects of market relationships that encourage them.)

Production of the positively valued feelings decreases for two reasons. First, the feelings are experienced less often directly, because behaviors that induce them occur less often. Second, there is an indirect effect in that it eventually becomes difficult to muster forth a certain behavior that one has lost practice displaying, even during occasions when one otherwise might wish to do so. Constant repetition of self-interested behavior gradually tends to produce a general attitude of self-interest; constant repetition of impersonal behavior gradually tends to produce a general attitude of coldness. Even when one might wish to induce the positive feelings that come from behaving in an altruistic or warm way, one has, like the adult who hasn't played piano since childhood, trouble bringing it off. Attitudes encouraged *because of the very fact that markets exist* thus influence behavior, a process that runs counter to the standard assumption in microeconomic theory that preferences are formed exogenously to the market itself.

We may begin by looking at personalized relationships. Personalized relationships are ones where the identity of the person with whom one interacts is important. They may be contrasted with impersonal relationships, where the person's identity is unimportant.

Positively valued feelings are associated with personalized relationships for several reasons. First, such relationships are the appropriate forum for those feeling-inducing behaviors that can only be performed in a social context. Examples of such behaviors are giving praise, showing liking, and so forth. The feelings induced by such behaviors can have great value both for the giver (who enjoys the opportunity to express, say, praise) and for the receiver (who enjoys the opportunity to be the object of praise). An impersonal expression of praise (that is, one going to some random person for no particular reason) would be seen as nearly worthless by most people. The more relationships are impersonal, the fewer are the opportunities for displaying feeling-inducing

behavior and thus the fewer the positively valued feelings produced. Sharing positively valued feelings induced in a social context is also an important way to develop bonds among people. The
bonds in question in turn produce feelings such as trust and liking.

Second, personal relationships are also ones where we have the
possibility of achieving increased feelings of self-esteem because,
unlike the situation in impersonal relationships, we have the possibility of being valued "for our own sakes." We tend to attribute
a higher value to "learning for its own sake" than to an equivalent
amount of studying "just" to get good grades. We scorn a book
collection developed to adorn a sittingroom and impress visitors,
while cherishing one, consisting of the same books, developed to
be read and pondered over. Genuine love between two people
is precious, but a love based on the desire of one party to get the
other's wealth is tawdry. The importance of this distinction was,
of course, central to the moral philosophy of Kant, the second
formulation of whose categorical imperative stated that one should
always "act so that you treat humanity, whether in your own
person or in that of others, always as an end and never as a means
only."[26] We do not always value people for their own sakes in
personal relationships, of course, but at least the *possibility* of
doing so is there, where in impersonal relationships it is not.

Achieving the full efficiency benefits of markets requires that
interactions in market exchange be impersonal. This is because
if personal interactions *were* necessary, the scope for market production and allocation would be reduced to a small circle of people
who could have personal relationships with each other. An efficient
market requires large numbers of producers, buyers, and sellers.
It thus must be impersonal. Firms seeking to expand their markets
and consumers seeking a "better deal" for the things they buy are
all impelled to widen the network of people they deal with. If I
stay with a certain supplier of a product, not because he provides
the best value for the money, but because I am a personal friend,
market exchange becomes more personal, but at the cost of hurting
competitive price formation. (In effect, product differentiation has
created opportunity for monopoly.) Many of the people I deal
with at the marketplace must be people I have never seen before
and will never see again. Similarly, efficient markets impel a
division of labor where most things people buy are produced by
others they never met and who will never meet them. (Division
of labor, of course, is not unique to market systems, but efficiency

considerations provide a special incentive for it, as long as there are efficiency gains to be achieved thereby, in market situations.) Finally, the use of money in market exchange depersonalizes interactions as well, because money is an abstract, "dead" means of exchange that, unlike any specific good which incorporates the human effort put into its production, has no direct connection with human effort. The Marxist notion of alienation may be understood as involving the separation of the producer from any opportunity to receive recognition from the user for the product of his labor. The impersonal relationships of market exchange would appear to be what Marx had in mind when he wrote that in the marketplace "there is a definite social relation between men, that assumes . . . the fantastic form of a relation between things."[27]

In impersonal relationships, the value of the things being exchanged must itself be sufficient to make the exchange worthwhile, since the relationship imparts nothing of value. By contrast, in many nonmarket relationships, the opportunity the interaction generates to display feeling-inducing behavior is a *major* value. A classic example is the gift exchanges in primitive societies investigated by such anthropologists as Marcel Mauss and Bronislaw Malinowski.[28] Reciprocal gift-giving was frequently used to initiate friendship ties (for example, among groups living on different islands) or cement an emotional bond among the gift exchangers (for example, between families being united by marriage). Goods were transferred through the gift exchanges described by Mauss and Malinowski, but what was important in the interaction was not so much the specific identity of the things transferred as the interaction itself. Similarly, when one neighbor bakes a cake for another, the value of the interaction comes in significant measure from the display of feeling-inducing behavior.

It is in this context that many people fear that introducing elements of market exchange into human interactions will reduce them to impersonal market relationships and thus destroy a significant part of their value. Imagine, for instance, that I am staying at a friend's house and have an early plane to catch that requires me to leave the house at seven in the morning. The taxi to the airport costs $10. My friend typically leaves the house at half-past seven and his route takes him near the airport. If a firm with its headquarters in the apartment building where he lives said they needed to get a parcel dropped off at the airport, the friend would be willing to leave the house half an hour earlier to do so for a payment of $8. It would thus appear that there would be gains from trade if I offered my friend anywhere between $8 and $10 to get up half an hour earlier and drive me to the airport. Yet few people would ever offer the friend money to do so, reflecting a fear of the impact of such a step on the quality of the relationship between the two friends.[29]

Malinowski also noted in his study of gift exchange in some primitive tribes that the things exchanged had little practical value themselves.[30] Apparently the fear was that using goods that were themselves valuable might make the gift exchange resemble market exchange too much, with the attendant impersonality that would have devastated the feelings the exchange induced. Similarly, many people in our own society are hesitant about giving money (or even something practical that might have been bought by the recipient anyway) as a birthday or wedding gift. We similarly hesitate to sell a gift, although we would not hesitate to resell something we bought. Again, the fear is that introducing market relationships into ones that induce feelings injures the latter. Just as adding salt to fish draws the water from the fish and leaves it dry, so we fear that adding market relationships to feeling-laden ones will draw the feeling out of them and leave them dry.

The impersonality of interactions in market exchange constitutes one of the most hoary—but not for that less important—criticisms of the market. Lack of practice at personalized relationships can eventually produce an attitude of coldness, where people have difficulty mustering feeling-inducing behavior in themselves or reacting to it in others even when they want to. They thus come to have difficulty experiencing feelings at all. This imposes an additional cost.[31] Lacking opportunity to develop personal bonds with others, people feel lonely and distrustful—feelings induced by the absence of such bonds. (It should be noted that, in contrast to private nonmarket production and allocation decisions, governmental systems tend to have many impersonal features as well.)

Ironically, failure to develop trust as a result of lack of personalized relationships even has negative consequences for the functioning of market exchange itself. It was first noted by Durkheim in *The Division of Labor in Society* that preexisting interpersonal trust is important wherever using the market involves a time lapse between a promise to deliver something and its actual delivery.[32] More recently, Kenneth Arrow has argued that trust radically decreases transaction and policing costs, thus making many bargains possible that would not otherwise have been possible.[33]

The consequences of impersonal relationships are intensified because, for the market to work efficiently, people selling or buying the same thing must be in competition with each other. Note the difference between impersonal relationships and competition. People involved in market exchange *with each other* at least do interact, albeit impersonally, and do, at least fleetingly when they are involved in the exchange, share the common goal of achieving gains from trade. However, producers offering *the same thing* on the market must not interact with each other at all if the efficiency benefits of the market are to be fully realized. They must compete against each other, trying to gain at another's expense. (The same applies to workers.) Adam Smith's oft-cited remark about businessmen never meeting together even for a social occasion without hatching a conspiracy against the public interest is not only a statement about monopoly, but also a chilling expression about the lack of relationships among competitors that is required if the market is to function efficiently. This lack of contact with others, or even hostility towards them, exacerbates the problems of coldness, loneliness, and distrust that impersonal relationships already promote.

We move now to behaviors that induce positive feelings. There are positively valued feelings associated with spontaneity and altruism. Yet market exchange punishes these behaviors and hence decreases their production.

As discussed earlier in a different context, altruism is a behavior that can induce positive feelings both in the person behaving in an altruistic way and in the beneficiaries of altruism. Selfish behavior fails to induce such feelings. Altruism, by definition, can only be displayed in interactions with others. It is, indeed, one of the feeling-inducing behaviors that may be displayed in personal relationships. Earlier, I discussed the negative effect on the production of altruism of a social statement endorsing self-interest as a motivation in reducing pollution. Here, attention will be focused on the negative effect of market exchange on the production of altruism.

To act spontaneously is to act explicitly without full consideration of all the consequences, to "plunge ahead," to do "what seems right at the time," to "let go." Unlike altruism, spontaneity is a behavior we may demonstrate either by ourselves or in interactions with others. The opposite of spontaneity is calculation, whereby one acts as a rational maximizer—listing valued things, weighing them, and calculating what choice will bring about the greatest attainment of desired things. When one acts spontaneously, sometimes no consequences of the action are considered but the joy of the act itself. An overweight person on a diet acts spontaneously when he sees a luscious slab of strawberry shortcake with whipped cream in front of him—and devours it. In another case, a person acting spotaneously might consider only the most obvious consequences and ignore less obvious ones. Frequently, the spontaneous act brings benefits in the present and leads to costs in the future.

To put it mildly, spontaneous behavior is not an unmixed blessing. Often, the ignored negative consequences of spontaneity are experienced by others, as when a gang of teenagers spontaneously slashes tires or throws rocks at windows. One may also, by contrast, calculate in pursuit of altruistic goals. An extreme pattern of spontaneity in personal life becomes what Banfield calls "pathological present orientation," involving inability to sacrifice any present discomforts for future satisfaction.[34] Yet, independent of various positive and negative consequences of acting without full consideration of all the consequences of a choice, spontaneous behavior itself tends to induce more positively valued feelings than calculating behavior. First, in some people the act of choosing spontaneously may produce a feeling of exhilaration, analogous to the exhilaration that any risk taking produces. Second, spontaneity is for many people associated with more joy than calculation. The word "spontaneous" conjures in many people's minds the image of a person laughing or dancing, while the word "calculative" conjures someone sitting down with a dour expression on his face. This association remains for many people despite the fact that the spontaneous person may wake up in the morning after his night of abandon with a painful hangover, and the calculative person may become very happy when at some later time his calculations pay off. Nevertheless, once the association exists, it takes on a life of its own. Any spontaneous behavior is awarded an increment of joyful feelings, over and above any joyful consequences of the behavior, simply by virtue of its being spontaneous, and any calculated act is penalized a decrement of joylessness simply by virtue of its being calculative. Third, calculation is associated in many people's minds with selfishness. The association must be empirical, since there is no logical reason to believe that one cannot calculate on behalf of altruistic goals. Perhaps the empirical connection is seen to exist because of a recognition that self-interest tends to be a stronger motivation in most people than altruism. Summoning forth altruism may be seen as being difficult enough so that most people won't pay the further cost of calculating how best to be altruistic. Calculation on behalf of self-interest, by contrast, allows further net benefits to oneself. To the extent that people regard selfishness negatively, they thus tend to regard calculation negatively.

Calculation may, furthermore, induce choices that underproduce attainment of positively valued feelings because of the nature of calculation as a reasoning process. The reasoning process in rational maximizing behavior is an unemotional one, emphasizing cool rather than passionate judgment. In principle, positively valued *emotions* should be included and given the full weight one attributes to them in the objective function to be maximized, just like any other positively valued things. Yet what is possible in principle may be nearly unattainable psychologically. Most people do not make the watertight separation that exists in the rational choice model between the calculating process itself and the valued things about which one calculates. The novels—from Dickens's *Hard Times* to Flaubert's *Sentimental Education*—that present characters who were calculating present them as cold and devoid of feeling altogether. When a former speechwriter for President Carter criticized the Carter presidency for being "passionless," he, in effect, argued that the calculative style of the decision making in the White House drained consideration of passion-laden values out of decisions made.[35] A reasoning process without emotion will tend to shortchange consideration of valued emotions when choices are made.

Finally, tradeoffs between the present and the future are not objectively established. Yet the very process of calculation, when frequently repeated, tends to influence people towards attributing relatively greater weights in the choice process to future, rather than to present, benefits and less to more immediate consequences. It is easy to see why this is the case for any particular process of calculation. Any individual act of calculation involves, by definition, entry into one's objective function of things that otherwise would not have been considered. Since the smallest weight that a factor could have in a calculated choice is zero, and since nonconsideration inevitably would have involved attribution of a zero weight, the calculation process, simply by entering a thing into the objective function, tends to increase the weight attributed it compared to a situation where it was not considered at all. But something more than this takes place after frequent calculations. It requires an act of will to keep less immediately obvious consequences in general and future consequences in particular on our minds in the face of the natural tendency to think mainly about the obvious and the immediate. This act of will required for calculation tends gradually to get transferred into an increased weight ascribed in general to less immediately obvious goals. While one might originally have decided, even after considering both the present benefit, P, and the future cost, F, of an action, that it was worth paying F to get P, one might well, after frequent calculations, come to weight F heavily enough so that one chooses to forego P. Calculation, which was supposed to register preferences, ends up influencing them. This imposes a cost by making it difficult to give high weight, say, to the present, even when one might otherwise want to. This is seen in the complaint of the person who might lament he wishes he could just enjoy the present sometimes, instead of always thinking about future consequences all the time.

One connection between advocacy of widespread, unfettered markets and promotion of self-interested and calculative behavior is historical. The industrial revolution saw both an expansion of market exchange and, in the opinion of many contemporaries, an increase in self-interested and calculative behavior among people. This was, of course, one of the main themes of the literature of the period. Novels dealing with merchants or industrialists often portrayed them as hard-hearted, uncaring, or calculative. Prudence and rationality were regarded as the "bourgeois virtues." The Romantic movement in literature lamented the spread of calculation and nostalgically looked back to nature as an embodiment of a nonmarket, spontaneous world.

As in history, so in the history of ideas. Adam Smith built the case that, with universal and unfettered markets, the pursuit of self-interest would be harnessed to lead to a maximization of social welfare, not to the social disaster that moral philosophers had traditionally believed. And neoclassical economics has postulated, and prescribed, rational maximization as the process of individual choice. They have postulated it by arguing that people act "as if" they are maximizing attainment of some objective function, albeit imperfectly articulated, whenever they make choices. They have prescribed it by urging people to be more explicit about the calculating process if they wish to make decisions that will better maximize attainment of things they value.

That the spread of the market was historically associated with increased calculation and self-interest and that market advocates preach calculation and self-interest do not themselves demonstrate any deductive connection between market exchange and such behavior. A logical connection does exist, however, for several reasons.

The first involves incentives arising out of market exchange. A producer who behaves altruistically or spontaneously while others don't, thus adding to his relative costs, will be driven out of a competitive marketplace because his products cost more. This constitutes, of course, nothing else but the famous "discipline" of the market that punishes the slothful capitalist who fails to calculate as assiduously as his competitors and is thereby driven out of business. If things are allocated only on the market, a person seeking those things will suffer in terms of receiving less of the things being allocated or being charged more for them if he behaves spontaneously or altruistically in the market while those with whom he interacts behave calculatingly or self-interestedly. This is because others will take advantage of him. The person who spontaneously puts down whatever money he has in his pocket for something that takes his fancy will generally pay more to the calculating person with whom he is dealing than the person who calculates and bargains.[36] An altruistic person interacting with a selfish one will always give and never get. A further additional cost of spontaneity in such situations comes from the resentment (a negatively valued feeling) one experiences from being taken advantage of by somebody else. By contrast, if one suffers certain costs due to a spontaneous act involving oneself only, resentment is not felt. (People tend to take the attitude that they did it to themselves.) Additionally, altruistic behavior may produce negatively valued feelings of rage or disappointment for the person so acting when displayed for the benefit of another person who turns out to be self-interested. Such results occur if others prefer to behave calculatingly or self-interestedly, and also if others would have preferred to behave spontaneously or altruistically, but only if an agreement could be reached guaranteeing everyone's behavior so that nobody suffers from anybody else's spontaneity or altruism. By contrast, if a thing is produced or allocated by nonmarket methods, a person may behave spontaneously or altruistically without paying a further price in terms of inability to continue production or of receiving less of that thing.

The second connection between market exchange and calculatingness or self-interest is that, in market relationships, gains from trade are normally expected for each exchange. This encourages calculation in order to determine whether such gains are present. In ongoing personal relationships, such as friendships for example, the gains for each party are longer term and much less tied to any particular interaction. This relieves friends of the pressure to calculate about benefits and costs each time they interact, and it gives people practice in behaving in ways that do not produce immediate gains for themselves—good training in the road towards altruism.

Third, prices discourage spontaneity by making losses from it more visible and, similarly, encourage calculation by decreasing the effort it requires. If a person goes out and buys a mink coat for $10,000 and proceeds to sell it on a whim for $100, the cost he pays for such spontaneity is plain. The costs of spontaneity are sometimes as clear, but sometimes they are not. If a person spontaneously gets drunk at get-togethers with the parents of his fiancée and she calls off the wedding, the costs of the spontaneity are indeed apparent, though nothing is expressed in market prices. If, however, a man meets a beautiful woman at a sailors' bar and spontaneously presents her with a pendant his mother gave him on her deathbed, the exact cost of the spontaneity is more difficult to establish. Furthermore, as anyone who has tried benefit-cost analysis knows, it is easier to calculate how one maximizes attainment of a diverse set of goals if they can all be measured in a common monetary metric.

As for production of altruism, market exchange discourages it by reducing the scope for personal relationships where altruism may be most fittingly displayed. Also, as Locke recognized in his *Second Treatise on Government*, the use of money, the medium of exchange in markets, ends any natural limitations placed on the rewards for self-interest by providing a source of value that doesn't spoil.[37]

The increased costs the external environment imposes for spontaneous or altruistic behavior when the market is used decrease production of such behavior. Furthermore, as noted earlier, through repeated practice, attitudes of calculatingness and self-interest tend to develop. This imposes a cost by making it difficult to act spontaneously or altruistically even when one might otherwise wish to. Laments such as "I wish I could just act spontaneously sometimes, but I can't," or "I wish I weren't so stingy, but I can't help it," illustrate the attitude-formation process. Unlike the case of impersonal interaction, where alternative behaviors were not punished but simply not practiced, such attitude formation is hastened in the cases of spontaneity and altruism by the extra punishment one has suffered for such behavior. It is analogous to the fox who dismissed the grapes as sour because he couldn't have gotten them anyway. The example of the hard-bitten person who states he has learned a lesson about altruism from the "school of hard knocks" is a familiar one. Once burned, twice cautious.

The argument that market exchange punishes spontaneous and altruistic behavior should not be misinterpreted as a statement that, in the absence of market exchange, calculation or self-interest would or should not exist. Both individual personality dispositions and the inevitable costs of spontaneous behavior place limits on its extent, even without the further discouragement that market exchange provides. Behavior that never takes one's own future into account imposes serious costs. Powerful psychological drives guarantee significant self-interested behavior with or without market exchange. Furthermore, given the inevitable existence of calculation and self-interest, it is to the credit of markets as a mechanism for steering production and allocation that they can harness calculation and self-interest in the service of increased production of goods that then can be allocated. It is all very fine to speak, as I did earlier, of the advantages of nonmarket mechanisms as ones that do not discourage spontaneity and altruism. But a production system that did not know how to harness inevitable calculatingness and self-interest might have few goods produced. All that is being argued is that many people might well want spontaneity and altruism to be keys on the keyboard of behaviors available for use, and believe that preserving a place for them on the keyboard may require limiting the domain for the market.

Another objection to the line of argument presented here might be that any time we interact with other people in a spontaneous

or altruistic way—and not only when we do so in market contexts—
the risk exists that we can be taken advantage of by others acting
calculatingly or self-interestedly. (This objective applies more to
market exchange than to market competition in production.) This
is true, but it ignores the loss in ability to be selective that occurs,
to the extent that supplies of goods one wants are allocated only
via impersonal exchange. In personalized relationships, we know
enough about the other people we interact with to display altruism
and spontaneity to those we feel won't take advantage of it. If we
value the feelings induced by spontaneous or altruistic behavior
highly, we will choose as people to interact with mainly those
who won't take advantage of our behavior. If we must enter into
impersonal relationships, we enter into situations where we don't
know enough about people to know whether they will take advantage of us. Continued spontaneous or altruistic behavior under
such circumstances is what sets up a person for a fall.

The Downvaluation Effect

I will now turn from this discussion of feeling-inducing behaviors
to the second broad category of psychological cost imposed by
using the market to steer production and allocation. This cost
involves a direct reduction in the perceived value of a thing (willingness to pay) due to market exchange and price setting itself.
The very act of putting behavior on the market or placing a price
on something may make us value it less. Just as failing to stigmatize
polluting behavior may decrease the level of environmental quality
society chooses to attain by making the value ascribed to a clean
environment less than it would otherwise be, so placing a price
on environmental quality by setting a charge for pollution may
accomplish the same end by lowering that value as well.

Examples of the perceived cheapening of a thing's value by the
very act of buying and selling it abound both in everyday life and
in everyday language. The horror and disgust that accompany the
idea of buying and selling human beings is based on the sense
that this would dramatically diminish human worth. Praise that
is bought is worth little, even to the person buying it. "He pros-
tituted himself" and "He's a whore" said of people who have sold
something reflect the view that certain things shouldn't be sold
because doing so diminishes their value. Thus condemnation is
heaped on those responsible for such diminution.

Item: When a certain professor of economics retired to another academic community and complained that he was having trouble making friends, a critical colleague in his new community suggested to him, "Why don't you buy yourself one?"

Item: In its 1978 Christmas gift catalogue, according to *The New York Times*, the Sakowitz department store in Houston "offered in its Christmas catalogue what was described as a tongue-in-cheek 'ultimate gift' of Walter Cronkite as a dinner guest. . . . The Sakowitz catalogue offered well-heeled Texans and others a chance to pay $94,125 to present a gift of a dinner party with 'worldly friends like Walter Cronkite' " and a list of others. Cronkite was not amused. He "filed suit in Houston demanding that Sakowitz not only remove his name from its catalogue but also 'notify all persons, customers, news organizations and any other groups or entities to whom it has sent the catalogue' that he's not really ready to break bread with just anybody for a price."[38]

Item: In an article discussing the strategy of the Carter Administration in trying to seek ratification of the SALT arms limitation agreement, the *National Journal* wrote:[39]

> *Many assume that when the crunch comes, Carter will do nearly anything to win the last few crucial votes.* [An article in the journal Foreign Policy *stated that*], "In his intimate encounters with Senators on the Panama treaties, Carter revealed a propensity to mingle low politics with high policy, to link allusions to public works projects with discussions of the nation's overriding interest in a peaceful hemisphere. A repetition of this tactic on SALT would ensure its defeat."
>
> . . . *Carter aides, however, vehemently deny these charges, saying that Carter would not reduce such a vital debate to that level of politics and that, even if he tried, the press would blow the whistle.*
>
> "We have looked favorably upon those who have supported us in the past; that is the essence of politics," said Robert Beckel. "But on an issue the magnitude of SALT, the basic lessons don't apply."

The first reason that placing something on the market decreases its perceived value should be apparent from the previous discussion. If a good becomes less associated with the production of positively valued feelings because of market exchange, the good loses in perceived value to the extent those feelings are valued. The costs of decreased production of feelings due to market exchange thus rub off on goods exchanged on the market. This can be seen clearly in instances where a thing may be transferred both by market and nonmarket mechanisms. The willingness to pay for sex bought from a prostitute is less than the perceived value of sex that consummates love. (Imagine the reaction if a practitioner of benefit-cost analysis, in the constant pursuit of market prices that can be attributed to things not normally bought and sold in markets, computed the benefits of sex in our society based on the price of prostitute services!)

This is true for another reason. If one values the existence of a nonmarket sector because of its connection with production of certain valued feelings, then one ascribes added value to any nonmarketed thing simply as a representative for, and part repository of, values represented by the nonmarket sector one wishes to preserve. This status removed, the thing loses its repository character and, hence, part of its perceived value. This seems certainly to be the case for things in nature such as pristine streams or undisturbed forests: for many people who value them, part of their value comes from their position as repositories of values the nonmarket sector embodies.

There is a second way that placing something in the market may decrease its perceived value. The market is a realm of inequality, where rewards are not equal and goods are not shared equally. For someone who values equality, a thing may be valued more highly simply because it is such that it can be shared equally among all citizens. Thus, part of the perceived value of things as varied as our national parks and our right to vote would appear to be their very character as part of a common treasure that we all share equally. That is, part of their value is as a repository for the value ascribed to equality. Such equal sharing would not occur if those things were placed in the market; it is possible only through nonmarket allocation. Placing such things in the market would thus tend to decrease their perceived value.

The other ways that placing a price on something may decrease its perceived value involve ways that one is able to proclaim the special value of something simply by keeping it outside the system of markets and prices of which most valued things form a part. Emile Durkheim noted in *The Elementary Forms of Religious Life* that a key element of religion was the separation of a small subset of things adjudged "sacred" from the larger category of things that were "profane."[40] That separation was signalled, Durkheim noted, by treating sacred things in ways that the run of things were not normally treated. Animals are normally eaten, but sacred animals are not. Ground can normally be used for farming or for building shelter, but sacred ground is not. The very act of keeping something outside the realm of the market, then, is a way of proclaiming its special value: most things are bought and sold, but special things are not.

Beyond this general phenomenon, there are specific statements, which can only be made about nonmarketed things, that serve to enhance, affirm, and protect their value. These include the statements that a thing is "not for sale" or is "priceless." Market goods cannot be proclaimed to be "not for sale," since things on the market by definition are for sale. And buying and selling something leads of necessity to the attachment of an explicit price to it.

Proclaiming a thing "not for sale" is a way of showing that the thing is valued for its own sake. In another context above, the special value attributed to things valued for their own sakes was discussed. By contrast, any time somebody sells a thing for money, he demonstrates that the thing sold was valued only instrumentally and not for its own sake. Furthermore, the common run of goods is exchangeable for other goods of an unrelated nature. To state that something cannot be transferred in that way places it in an exceptional category. One requires a person interested in obtaining that thing to be able to offer something else from that sphere in particular, rather than making available to him the easier alternative of obtaining the thing for goods or money that can have been obtained in an infinity of ways. This enhances its value. If I am willing to say, "You're a really kind person" to whomever pays me to do so, my praise loses the value that attaches to it from being exchangeable only for an act of kindness. There is an interesting doctrine in contract law that it is considered to be an unacceptable threat (duress) to get somebody to accept certain contract terms by saying that if the other party does not accept the terms, one will turn the individual in to the police for a crime the other committed. The notion behind the doctrine would appear to be that involving the institution of the law in an exchange outside its own sphere cheapens the institution's value. Place a "not for sale" sign next to something and one thus becomes like the Fairy Godmother waving her magic wand in *Cinderella:* pumpkins are turned to coaches and tattered rags to a splendid gown.[41]

Also, if there is something we have already decided we value very highly, one way of stamping the thing with a cachet affirming its high value is to announce that it is "not for sale." Such an announcement does more, however, than just relect—and affirm— a preexisting high valuation. It signals a thing's distinctive value to others and helps us exhort them to value the thing more highly than they otherwise might. And it also expresses our resolution to safeguard that distinctive value. To state that something is "not for sale" is thus also a source of value for that thing, since if a thing's value is easy to affirm, to exhort others to recognize, or to proclaim a desire to safeguard, it will be worth more than an otherwise similar thing without such qualities. Like the ruby slippers the Good Witch Glenda gave Dorothy in *The Wizard of Oz* to guard her from harm, it protects something important from decay or attack.

The safeguarding function of proclaiming something "not for sale" is related to the notion of temptation. The idea that one might do something one didn't "really" want to do is a difficult one for the standard economic paradigm where if someone voluntarily accepted x in exchange for y, the person has become better off because the choice shows a preference for x over y, and therefore should be glad he had the opportunity to make the choice, no matter what the y is that he has given up.

In fact, though, there are several kinds of situations in which an individual might be worried about temptation and hence wish to keep a thing "not for sale." (In order to avoid temptation, the individual's preferred choice would be that an outright societal ban exist on selling the thing in question. If that is impossible, he would at least wish personally to proclaim it to be "not for sale.") He might fear that at some future moment he could act "in a moment of weakness" in a way that under normal circumstances he would not. We recoil in horror from the dread fear that if our liberties could be sold, or our ideals, or even our own parents, we might at some time sell them.[42] If the person actually "gives in" to temptation and acts in the way he was afraid of, he has suffered the loss of something normally valued. In particular, people are frequently worried about the dazzling power of money to get them to do things that they believe in a general sense they should not do. Much of the sentiment behind proverbs such as "The love of money is the root of all evil" arises from apprehensions about what one might do when wads of money are placed before one's eyes. If something that a person would normally not wish to sell has an ongoing price attached to it on a functioning market, long periods of steadfastness can be cancelled out by one moment where some special weakness causes him to exchange the valued thing. Even if we end up not giving in to temptation, one might wish a thing not to be for sale to avoid the anxiety costs of realizing that one might, at any time, give in. Note the implications of this analysis for the bias favoring looking at behavior rather than attitudes in the economic analysis of how much people value something. I once conducted a survey where people were asked whether they would rather accept $500 in cash to put up with a certain noise disturbance or have the noise quieted. Informed that most respondents stated they would prefer to have the noise quieted, an economist countered that it would be surprising if people would behave the same way "if the $500 were actually put in front of them" rather then "merely" answering a question about a hypothetical situation. This objection has some merit, but it should be noted that the *attitude* may express a person's reflective view and the *behavior*—with the $500 "in front of him"—a giving in to what he would regard as temptation. Under such circumstances, the attitude would appear, to me, at any rate, at least as genuine and perhaps more "genuine" an expression of preferences as the behavior.

One may be worried, not only by the fact that one might sell something that one normally wouldn't wish to (and thus have it gone), but by the price one might sell it for as well. If the proclamation is made that something is "not for sale," a once-and-for-all judgment has been of its special value. When something is bought and sold on the market, the issue of its perceived value is constantly being raised again and again, and a standing invitation is made to reconsider that original judgment. Were people constantly faced with questions such as "How much money could get you to give up your freedom of speech?" or "How much would you sell your vote for if you could?" the perceived value that the freedom to speak or the right to vote have would soon become devastated, as, in moments of weakness, people started saying "Maybe it's not worth *so much* after all." Better not to be faced with the constant questioning in the first place. Something similar did in fact occur when the slogan "Better Red than Dead" was launched by some pacifists during the Cold War. Critics pointed out that the very posing of this stark choice—in effect, "Would you *really* be willing to give up your life in exchange for not living under communism?"—reduced the value people attached to freedom and thus diminished resistance to attacks on freedom.

Given the negative feelings that accompany the very *thought* of selling something that one would ordinarily not wish to sell, the most tragic aspect of temptation may be the fact that once one allows oneself to be tempted, one may be better off giving in. Imagine a situation where the perceived net benefit from choosing to take x in exchange for y is one unit, while the pangs from just considering selling cost two units. Since these pangs are experienced whether the exchange is made or not, once the situation is clearly in front of you, you are better off taking the exchange than not taking it, because you "cut your losses" by at least making the exchange. But you are still one unit worse off than you otherwise would have been had the possibility of exchange never been presented. These are situations where the person would have preferred that thing x would never have been salable on the market.[43]

Finally, of some things valued very highly it is stated that they are "priceless," that "no price is too high" for them, or that they have "infinite value." This is not the case for all things which one might wish to proclaim are not for sale. Say a daughter has in her possession some inexpensive candlesticks used many years earlier by her long-dead mother. She might well wish to proclaim that they are not for sale as a way of affirming and protecting their value to her. But she probably wouldn't go so far as to use the word "priceless" or "of infinite worth" to describe them. Such expressions are reserved for a subset of things not for sale, such as life or health.

For an economist, to state that something is "priceless" or that "no price is too high" would be to state that one would be willing to trade off an infinite quantity of all other goods for one unit of the priceless good, a situation that empirically appears highly unlikely. Economists thus tend to scoff at talk of "pricelessness." What economists miss when they so scoff is the effect that the very attachment of the word "priceless" has regarding the thing to which the word is applied. The word "priceless" may ring silly to an economist's ears, but to most people it is pregnant with meaning; calling something "priceless" thus serves, analogously in effect but independently in action to the proclamation that something is not for sale, to affirm and protect the value of the thing to which it is attributed.

The value-affirming and value-protecting functions cannot be bestowed to expressions that merely denote attribution of a determinate, albeit high, valuation. John F. Kennedy in his inaugural address proclaimed that the nation was ready to "pay any price (and) bear any burden . . . to assure the survival and the success of liberty." Had he stated instead (as most economists probably would have preferred) that we were willing to "pay a high price" or "bear a large burden" for liberty, the statement would have rung hollow.

An economist might reply that people do not always "behave" as if they believe things called "priceless" really are so. On a grand level, we do not spend unlimited resources to save a human life. On a more mundane level, we refrain from speaking our minds freely out of deference or fear. However, behavior in different contexts is different; a person who in everyday life might refrain from speaking his mind freely out of simple deference might lay down his life if a tyrant tried to silence him at the point of a gun. Opponents of stricter regulation of health risks often argue that we show by our daily risk-taking behavior that we do not value life infinitely, and therefore our public decisions should not reflect the high value of life that proponents of strict regulation propose. However, an alternative view is equally plausible. Precisely because we fail, for whatever reasons, to give lifesaving the value in everyday personal decisions that we in some general terms believe we should give it, we may wish our social decisions to provide us the occasion to display the reverence for life that we espouse but do not always show. Indeed, a statement that something is priceless is a form of behavior as well. All this is another particular illustration of the general point that preferences are not fixed, but vary in different contexts.

When a thing previously called priceless is given a price, its value is diminished. This is true in the trivial, though important, sense that any determinate price is less than priceless. But this is also true because of the value-affirming and value-protecting functions of the notion of pricelessness. The option of attributing pricelessness to something is available only for nonmarket goods. Once generally traded on a market, a Rembrandt painting or a Hope diamond may still be quite valuable, but they can no longer be called priceless. Among those things we value very highly, we are able to call liberty, human life, health, or unspoiled nature priceless and not Rembrandts or diamonds because the latter are explicitly bought and sold while the former are not. Even if one did not oneself buy and sell the thing, the fact that others do so removes the "priceless" label from it. And even occasional sale of something that one would wish to regard as priceless can be damaging. To the person who states that human life is priceless can always be made the reply that the Mafia price for a contract to kill a man is $5,000.

The Appropriate Scope for Markets

So much for the psychological costs of markets. It might be noted that there also may exist psychological benefits of using the market. A person who feels that spontaneity or present-orientation are excessively prevalent in people might favor markets precisely *because* they encourage calculation and future-orientation. Early proponents of capitalism argued that capitalism promoted thrift, something they regarded as virtue in itself, independent of any positive consequences it had, because they regarded the very ability to abstain from present enjoyment as a virtue. Furthermore, it was also argued that, in comparison with alternative forms of allocation such as plunder, the market represented a benign form of human interaction.[44] Similarly, impersonal relationships might be welcomed by those who fear they will be excluded from any means of getting things otherwise—say, minority groups, or anyone with personal characteristics unpleasing to others. (In the marketplace a black is able to say, "My money is as good as yours.") And the division of labor in society that is part of the efficiency benefits of markets also, in the view of Emile Durkheim, is a force that makes people more dependent on each other and thus increases ties among people.[45] Furthermore, a firm searching for things to produce for the market needs to have a good insight into what the desires of others, his potential customers, are—as any textbook in marketing emphasizes.[46] Such a search can increase production of feelings, if not of altruism, at least of empathy towards others. Finally, the market may lead to placing a higher valuation on something than would otherwise be the case. The attachment of a market price to something clearly signals its value; it is easier to ignore the value of something to which no price is attached. (Indeed, this very phenomenon lies behind accusations that using the market encourages materialism. This is partly because "materialism" is often considered merely another word for "selfishness," but also partly because a materialistic person is thought to be unable to see the value in things to which no price is attached.)

These potential psychological benefits of markets should be taken into consideration, of course, but it is important to note that they, just like the psychological costs discussed, tend to be left out of economists' analyses of the subject, which analyze market exchange simply in terms of its efficient properties and not as a form of human interaction.

One possible objection to this whole line of argument should be noted. The psychological costs of producing and allocating a thing using the market, it might be suggested, would presumably be reflected in a decreasing perceived value (willingness to pay) for the thing in the market as opposed to the value one would place on obtaining it through some nonmarket mechanisms where positively valued feelings would be produced and the thing would not suffer from having a money price attached to it. The efficiency benefits of producing and allocating it using the market would be reflected in a lower production cost. Both these factors would lower the market price of the good compared to the nonmonetary price one would have to pay under nonmarket mechanisms. An individual might himself then decide whether the benefits in terms of a lower price he would pay getting the good in the market were worth the psychological costs of participation in the market.

Even were it the case that the considerations adduced here implied no case for societal intervention in the scope of markets, they would at a minimum help explain why individuals who value highly the feelings whose production decreases because of market exchange or the ability to affirm and enhance a thing's value by keeping it off the market would themselves wish to restrict the scope of their own market participation. Their choices will now appear more understandable. Also, we will be able to understand why people with such values might seek to exhort others to reduce the scope of their market participation.

Several problems arise with the argument that such decisions may solely be left to individual choices, however. First, decisions about whether to integrate a previously nonmarketed thing into the market system sometimes can be made only at the societal level. Such is the case with environmental quality, the nonmarket thing directly under discussion here. Second, conceptually there is something of an infinite regress in asking someone to answer the question, "How much are you willing to pay not to have to think in terms of willingness to pay?" One must be uneasy about any intellectual system that makes it conceptually impossible to escape from its premises. Third, if no societally established mechanisms for allocation of a good (such as gratis distribution or rationing) exist, then the choice confronting the person who desires the good is between buying it on the market and getting it through some voluntary nonmarket allocation. Some organized voluntary system of nonmarket allocation, if there were no transaction costs to organize it, might be less expensive than the market—the psychological benefits would outweigh the increased economic cost of production. Yet the transaction costs of organizing a voluntary system of nonmarket allocation (such as collecting money from members of the system to purchase a quantity of the good in question for later nonmarket allocation) could well make the system more expensive than the market, and thus it would not develop. However, the marginal transaction costs for the government, which is already in place and has a tax system to collect money, of organizing a nonmarket allocation system are much less, and this might make such a system the cheapest one. Assuming the government made it compulsory to participate in such an organized nonmarket allocation mechanism for a good, the benefits of establishing a compulsory system would outweigh the costs if the psychological savings from the compulsory system for those who preferred it to market purchase were greater than the efficiency losses for those who would have preferred market purchase to nonmarket allocation.

Precluding social decisions also implies preventing individuals from dealing with the problem of temptation in the most effective way. One might, it will be remembered, wish to avoid temptations either to sell a thing one doesn't really want to sell or to engage in market exchange that will have long-run attitude-forming effects such as development of coldness or calculativeness. Although one may try to avoid temptation by an act of will (including the personal proclamation that a thing is "not for sale"), the surest way of preventing temptation is through a societal decision keeping some things off the market entirely.[47]

Finally, important parts of the psychological costs of market participation affect others in addition to the person who is making the choice. (The choice, in other words, has external effects.) Most of the feeling-inducing behaviors whose production is decreased when the market is used are behaviors that, in part, make *other* people feel good. If I am involved in a personal relationship where I express praise to another, I may feel good by expressing the praise. But the object of my praise feels good as well. If I am altruistic, others benefit. If these behaviors are not produced, others suffer.

Similarly, others suffer if a person buys and sells on the market things that the others wish to keep not for sale. Such things, as noted earlier, can then no longer meaningfully be referred to as "priceless." And the reduction in perceived value may occur even if an individual makes a personal decision not to put the valued thing up for sale. When we condemn Esau for selling his birthright for a mess of pottage, or a woman for prostituting herself, we are accusing them of deciding to value the things in question so cheaply—we think, for instance, a birthright is worth much more than a mess of pottage. But if all that was involved were a criticism for faulty evaluation of how much something was worth, the condemnation would hardly be as severe as it is. We may regard somebody who sells a brand new Mercedes for $10 as foolish or lacking judgment, but we do not condemn him morally. The stronger condemnation originates in the effect their action has on the perceived value for *us* of the thing sold.

There is also the question of the kind of society we live in, that is, the distribution of preferences people have. People might well wish to live in a society with a high production of positively valued feelings, or where many people assign certain particular things extremely high value, even beyond the effects of experiencing those feelings themselves or personally assigning the high value itself. People might be upset about the spread of selfishness or coldness in the society where they live even if they themselves amply experience altruism and warmth. People might be concerned if others assign a small value to certain feelings. Yet the contribution that any individual decision to participate in market exchange has on the total psychological costs that using the market imposes is infinitesimal. Under such conditions, it would not be rational for an individual to refrain from market participation to avoid the increment of psychological costs resulting from that particular abstinence. It would be rational to agree with others to prohibit using the market for production and/or allocation of certain goods so as to achieve a certain kind of society.

A final argument against always leaving decisions about the

scope of market participation to individual choice is that individuals may not be the best judges of the "true" value of the psychological costs they pay for the efficiency benefits of using the market, even insofar as these judgments affect only the person making the decision about market participation. The argument might be simply a paternalistic one that a person just "doesn't understand" how valuable are the feelings he is sacrificing to get a thing a few cents cheaper. But the argument may be more subtle than that. The value ascribed such feelings isn't fixed. Just as the sight of others selling for a song a thing we had considered very valuable will gradually tend to erode our own valuation of it, so may failure to experience frequently certain emotions gradually reduce the value ascribed them. One's preferences are clearly influenced by one's experiences. Just as many people worry that people who grow up in dictatorships will have trouble developing a taste for liberty because they've never experienced what it is like, we have grounds to fear that children growing up in a society where everything is bought and sold might have trouble developing tastes for feelings less common when the market is used. All societies act "paternalistically" to some significant extent in influencing the preferences of small children. In this case, the proposed influencing is quite benign: by prohibiting using the market in some instances, the intention is to *preserve* a situation where people have a range of preferences to choose among, not to decrease that range.

To the extent that these decisions should be social ones, standard economic analysis would counsel that what is needed is a benefit-cost analysis. The more things are removed from the market, the greater the efficiency losses. After a while as well, the marginal benefits of taking an additional thing off the market level off. What this suggests is that one might keep things off or remove things from the market until the point where marginal benefit of keeping them off or removing them equals the marginal cost. Strangely enough, however, in their brief discussion in *A Primer for Policy Analysis* of what they refer to as the criticism that "the market process in itself (is) unattractive," Edith Stokey and Richard Zeckhauser adopt an uncharacteristically nonmarginalist approach to this problem. "If it is to serve as the basis for a telling objection to the market system," the authors write, "we must be able to demonstrate that there is a more attractive system for allocating resources, one whose shortfall in performance relative

to a market system does not render it unacceptable."[48] The choice
is not either-or, but rather how much scope one wishes to give
the market. The thrust of the analysis here is that people may
desire, not total abolition of markets, but protection of *some* things
from production or allocation steering through markets, so that
the psychological costs market mechanisms exact will not be un-
acceptably high. If we do not recognize our own society as one
completely dominated by impersonal or competitive relationships,
or one where altruism or spontaneity have disappeared, or one
where we can say of nothing that it is "priceless"—this may well
be because some things have been kept out of the market. We
might wish that more things be taken out (if we think too great
a psychological cost is being paid) or we might wish to be careful
not to have more things put in (if we are worried about increasing
the psychological costs).

There are several possible criteria people might use for selecting
which things to keep off the market. Some have already been
suggested. Any thing whose value one wishes to give the affir-
mation and enhancement that keeping it off the market bestows
is a suitable candidate for being kept off.

Second, certain things are apt candidates for keeping off the
market because they have characteristics associated with experiencing feelings the production of which flourishes in nonmarket
contexts. This applies most dramatically to individual items that
have "emotional value" attached to them—such as family heir-
looms, souvenirs of happy occasions, and so forth. Since the
emotional value is individual, the decision to keep them off the
market is also best made individually. But such feeling-related
characteristics can also be experienced by large numbers of people
at the same time. For example, wild nature, both because of its
unplanned features and its radically different appearance from the
world of the city and of technology that is associated with calculation, becomes itself associated with spontaneity for many people, and is thus an apt candidate for keeping off the market.[49]

Finally, because creating a market in *anything* not previously
bought and sold on the market decreases production of valued
emotions, a criterion for not setting up a market in something
becomes simply that the thing has not been bought and sold on
the market previously, independent of any of its other characteristics. This was illustrated aptly in the case of discount coupons
that a number of airlines handed out as a promotional measure

during several weeks of 1979. The coupons were given to customers taking a flight on the airline during a certain period and could be used during a later period to obtain 50 percent price reductions on any flight the airline flew. A market developed where those who had received the coupons were offered cash for them, for resale to others. Nothing in the nature of the coupons themselves made them a likely candidate for protection from the effects of the market. The emotional value of the coupons was nil. They were not extraordinarily valuable in any other way. Yet many people reacted to the establishment of a market in these coupons with unease. *The New York Times* reported that "leading companies" in the travel business "frowned on the practice," with the head of one firm quoted as saying, "It's sleazy. It's not our business."[50]

Finally, a word ought to be said about the specific applicability of all this to using charges to steer production and allocation of pollution (and hence, environmental quality). Setting a charge means using prices to steer production and allocation, but when charges are used there is (in contrast to a marketable rights system where "rights" to emit a unit of pollution would actually be auctioned off and subject to resale) no direct market *exchange* of a thing called environmental quality. Instead, the charge ideally would be set by determining the price that would have resulted had there been market exchange.

The full-blown psychological costs of using the market occur in instances where prices are established *and* where market exchange (with the attendant decrease in production of positively valued feelings) occurs as well. These would be relevant in discussions of proposals by economists for greater reliance on the market in areas such as health care or education. They are not, at least conceptually, fully relevant to proposals for using charges in environmental policy (although they would be for marketable rights proposals). The costs in terms of decreased perceived value for things to which a price has been attached do, however, apply. Furthermore, the level of the charge is to be set through a calculative process that discourages spontaneity.

In conclusion, then, there are reasons for being concerned about the use of economic incentives in environmental policy out of a fear that "using the market" or establishing a price for pollution— and hence environmental quality itself—imposes costs.

Equity Considerations in the Design of Individual Programs

One possible grounds for concern about the use of economic incentives in environmental policy is that they would be inequitable because they would allow the rich to continue polluting and pay the charge, while those with less money would have no choice but to reduce pollution. Insofar as charges for air and water pollution are concerned, this view is based on an error of reasoning. When people make decisions about whether to undertake some activity that gives them satisfaction but also has a cost, their decisions are indeed based not only on their preferences (the degree of satisfaction the activity gives them) and on the relative price of the activity, but also on their budget constraints. It is true that increasing the price of some activity that gives people satisfaction will usually produce a greater decrease in its consumption by the poor than by the rich. But polluting behavior rarely gives polluters any satisfaction over and above the costs saved by not having to install abatement devices. If polluters are charged for pollution, it is rational for *any polluter, poor or rich,* to reduce polluting behavior up to the point where the savings from reducing the pollution equals the charge. There is thus no equity issue involved. The only way it could be otherwise would be if polluters gained satisfaction from the very act of polluting, a "satisfaction," beyond the cost savings, that the poor would likely give up before the rich.

It should be noted, however, that although the equity argument does not properly apply to charges for air and water pollution, it does apply to some other issues involving use of charges in environmental policy, such as increased tolls or parking surcharges (as opposed to parking bans) in transportation control plans. Furthermore, it applies to many other issue areas, such as energy pricing, where economists have played an important role in policy debates. Furthermore, most economists believe that individual public policies should not be designed with equity consideration in mind, with equity issues addressed only through general cash transfer payments. (This lack of sympathy with the importance of equity issues in the design of public policy in specific areas may explain why economists defending charges have not bothered to take on the error in the view that pollution charges allow the rich to continue polluting while making the poor stop; I have seen no response by economists to such contentions in the literature that advocates charges.)

Economists analyzing the place of equity considerations in the design of individual government programs generally conceptualize the question as a specific example of the general issue of cash vs. in-kind transfers as a means of income redistribution. Taking account of equity considerations in the design of individual programs is seen as an in-kind transfer, subject to the criticisms economists generally make of such transfers as an inefficient form of income redistribution.

There are many complex issues involved in any debate about the merits of cash vs. in-kind transfers. Since opposition to the use of charges in environmental policy based on equity considerations involves an error in reasoning, this issue will not be discussed at any length here. However, since the issue often is relevant to the use of economic incentives in other policy areas, brief consideration will be given to explaining why a person who believes equality to be an important value might favor consideration of equity issues in the design of individual programs, and not simply in the adoption of redistributive cash transfer payments.

A first reason for such a belief is an outgrowth of the view discussed earlier that the market is a domain of inequality and that part of the value of some unpriced things that are equally distributed comes out of their status as a repository for egalitarian values. Conversely, designing equality into some individual programs is a way of creating a *sphere* for the realization of strict equality that is not practically attainable in society as a whole. Considerations of production incentives and of just rewards for differential contributions or efforts—not to speak of the facts of heredity and environment—make general realization of equality of results among people neither practicable nor desirable. Nevertheless, if one gives the value of equality a strong weight, one may wish to see it realized in *some areas* of social life, even while realizing that it is unattainable as a general principle of social organization. No practical or desirable cash transfer would create such strict equality—because of the very fungibility of cash that is its advantage seen from the perspective of economic efficiency. Yet it is possible to realize the egalitarian ideal in some specific programs—to create a *domain of equality* that consecrates the value of equality while keeping its scope within practical and desirable limits.

A second reason to let equity considerations influence the design of individual programs is to promote development of individual preferences that assign equality a high weight. The average person, when he thinks about the plight of the disadvantaged (if he does so at all), does so in the context of specific problems that people face when they are disadvantaged—that they do not have enough to eat, or cannot pay their home heating oil bills, or that they land in highly risky jobs. Those who place a high weight on the value of equality would like to see people reminded of and thinking about the plight of the disadvantaged often and hard. They want to have equity considerations infuse the way people think about a whole range of problems, not just be shunted to a corner for consideration in the one context of considering the size of a cash transfer payment.

Furthermore, if equity considerations are considered only in a narrow context, it is likely that people, reminded of equity issues less often, will develop preferences that attach to equity a lower weight than if they were confronted with equity issues in many contexts; the total level of resources committed to improving the plight of the disadvantaged is thus likely to be less. The advocate of cash transfer is, in political debate, in effect constantly urging people to stifle natural inclinations of sympathy for the plight of others. He urges them instead to avoid taking account of equity in the given areas where it most naturally arises in people's minds—and instead, if they are interested, in some other time and place, to work for a cash transfer to the unfortunate. The result would be a sort of "I gave at the office" mentality, where people give and then don't think about the disadvantaged for the rest of the year. This would have negative effects on the strength of people's equity-related values.

A Note on the Choice Argument for Economic Incentives

The brunt of the argument of this chapter has been to contrast the efficiency advantages of economic incentives approaches to environmental regulation with the problems such an approach causes in other dimensions. I have ignored the nonefficiency related argument for economic incentive approaches—that they allow greater individual choice than does the use of standards. In this concluding section, I will deal briefly with that contention.

It is certainly reasonable to argue that expanding the arena for free choice and reducing the arena for intervention in one's choices by others tends to make people happier, because being able to choose for oneself is a source of satisfaction. Independent of its effects on satisfaction, the freedom to choose tends to be right because it gives expression to a respect for human dignity.[51] But the degree of free choice that people actually feel themselves as exercising will depend not only on the formal freedom to choose among alternatives, but also on the context of relative prices and individual budget constraints within which such choices are made. It has often been noted that poverty, for instance, may—to phrase it in the language of economics—put so many constraints on constrained maximization that the lyrical prose about "free to choose" may ring somewhat hollow. People may be "free to chose," but they may not feel as if they were. Something similar applies, I think, to sudden large shifts in the relative prices of goods as well. If the price of something one is used to buying is doubled overnight by a government decision to make the price of the good correspond to the social cost its consumption imposes, most people will experience such a price rise as something that "makes a mockery" (to use the phrase that would most likely be used in such a context) of free choice, just as poverty does in a different way. My own view is that much of the resentment at "government interference" in areas such as environmental regulation comes from the substantive changes that government policy seeks in the behavior of some individuals or organizations, changes that are not meant to be for the good of those whose behavior one is seeking to change, but for the good of other people who are victims of the external effects of such behavior. Bringing these changes about by making the undesired behavior considerably more expensive is somewhat less direct than ordering a reduction of the undesired behavior. It would probably reduce somewhat the resentment that comes from interfering with free choice. But I believe it would be an illusion to believe that those subjected to strong economic disincentives would suddenly feel that they had left the realm of coercion and entered the realm of freedom. Certainly, pollution charges no more than standards are "unanimous consent agreements" of the sort praised in discussions of voluntary exchange in the marketplace.

A somewhat related concern is that centralized decisionmaking by a bureaucracy, such as the standards approach represents, imposes greater inflexibility on the process than would a more "decentralized" economic incentives approach. Those who believe that an economic incentives approach is likely to be significantly less "rigid" than a standards approach may be disappointed as well. To be sure, for firms that do indeed change their behavior and choose to reduce their pollution less, while paying a charge for some of the pollution they would previously have abated, a charges system may be perceived as more flexible. (Happiness at the flexibility, however, may be outweighed by distress at the greater total payment that the combination of pollution abatement and charges on the pollution still emitted may require—a point to which I will return in the next chapter.) But charges introduce a new element of inflexibility into the system. A uniform charge on pollution will hit some firms and some industries very hard. Currently, those who are particularly badly hurt by a specific environmental standard—who may be put out of business, for instance—can attempt to make the case to bureaucrats and/or politicians for an extended compliance schedule or a variance. This set-up has both strong points and drawbacks, but whatever else one can say for it, at least one can say that it adds flexibility to the system. It would be far more difficult to "make an exception" to the obligation to pay a uniformly established charge. Again, this may be good or bad; most economists would argue that a firm that cannot sell its products at a profit after paying the social costs of the pollution it creates *should* go out of business. But whether it is good or bad, it certainly does not suggest that a charge system would be perceived as significantly more "flexible" than a standards system.

Endnotes

1. James Tobin, "On Limiting the Domain of Inequality," in E. S. Phelps (editor), *Economic Justice* (Harmondsworth: Penguin, 1973), p. 454.
2. Richard Posner, *Economic Analysis of Law*, 2nd edition (Boston: Little, Brown, 1977), pp. 111–16.
3. For exceptions, see Edmund S. Phelps, ed., *Altruism, Morality, and Economic Theory* (New York: Russell Sage, 1975). The connections of altruism and economic theory are also discussed in William M. Landes and Richard A. Posner, "Salvors, Finders, Good Samaritans, and Other Rescuers: An Economic Study of Law and Altruism," *Journal of Legal Studies*, 7 (January

1978); idem, "Altruism in Law and Economics," *American Economic Review*, 68 (May 1978).

4. Charles Fried, *Right and Wrong* (Cambridge: Harvard University Press, 1978), p. 32; idem, "Right and Wrong: Preliminary Considerations," *Journal of Legal Studies*, 5 (June 1976), p. 170.

5. Posner, op. cit., p. 173.

6. This example comes from Oliver Wendell Holmes, "Privilege, Malice, and Intent," *Harvard Law Review*, 8 (April 1899), pp. 10–12.

7. See the discussion on this in Lloyd Weinreb, *Criminal Law* (Mineola: The Foundation Press, 1975), pp. 468–80.

8. Oliver Wendell Holmes, *The Common Law* (Boston: Little, Brown, 1881), p. 3.

9. Rollin Perkins, *Criminal Law*, 2nd edition (Mineola: The Foundation Press, 1969), p. 739.

10. For a discussion, see John Hospers, *Human Conduct*, Shorter Ed. (New York: Harcourt Brace, 1972), Chs. 7–8.

11. Immanuel Kant, *Foundation of the Metaphysics of Morals* (Indianapolis: Library of Liberal Arts, 1959), p. 10.

12. For a discussion of this contention, see Hospers, op. cit., pp. 141–55.

13. Edmund S. Phelps, op. cit., p. 2.

14. Landes and Posner, op. cit.

15. This appears to be the view of Kenneth Arrow, in "Gifts and Exchanges," in *Ibid.*, pp. 351–52.

16. P. J. Fitzgerald, "Crime, Sin, and Negligence," *Law Quarterly Review*, 79 (1963), pp. 351–52.

17. Perkins, op. cit., p. 795.

18. M. R. Darby and E. Karni, "Free Competition and the Optimal Amount of Fraud," *Journal of Law and Economics*, 16 (April 1973); George Stigler, "The Optimum Enforcement of Laws," *Journal of Political Economy*, 78.

19. Mark Kelman, "Production Theory, Consumption Theory, and Ideology in the Coase Theorem," *Southern California Law Review*, 52 (March 1979).

20. See, for instance, Robert Kraynak, "John Locke: From Absolutism to Liberalism," *American Political Science Review*, 74 (March 1980).

21. This will be discussed further in Chapter 4.

22. The sum is the total level of pollution produced in society. Note the contrast between this approach and the approach used in cost-benefit analysis. It would be possible to come to results similar to those environmentalists come to, through a cost-benefit route, by assuming preferences that weight environmental quality very strongly—and such are, of course, the preferences environmentalists have.

23. Charles Dickens, *A Christmas Carol* (New York: Harper and Brothers, 1844), p. 5.

24. Charles Dickens, *Hard Times* (London: Chapman and Hall, 1858), pp. 206, 461.

25. These psychological costs should be distinguished from the costs, over and above the economic costs, that using the market imposes on those who lose at free competition. These costs are best noted in the context of a discussion of equity issues using the market raises.

26. Kant, op. cit., p. 47.
27. Karl Marx, *Capital* (New York: International Publishers, 1967), p. 72.
28. See Marcel Mauss, *The Gift* (New York: The Free Press, 1954); Cyril S. Belshaw, *Traditional Exchange and Modern Markets* (Englewood Cliffs: Prentice-Hall, 1965), particularly Ch. 2; and Peter P. Ekeh, *Social Exchange Theory: The Two Traditions* (Cambridge: Harvard University Press, 1974).
29. Another reason for the hesitation is that such a step would make the friend interchangeable with any other person interested in driving me to the airport—he is being chosen for the task because he's the cheapest one around to do it. Such interchangeability makes him not valued "for his own sake"— it diminishes my special valuation of him as my friend and his own self-image as a person I specially value.
30. Ekeh, op. cit., p. 25.
31. An individual might be afraid that he will not sufficiently take into account the impact of an individual decision to participate in market exchange on the long-term process of attitude formation. Such a fear relates to the notion of temptation, to be discussed in another context below, and also to the case for societal intervention regarding the scope for markets.
32. Emile Durkheim, *The Division of Labor in Society* (New York: The Free Press, 1964).
33. Arrow, in Phelps (ed.), op. cit.
34. Edward Banfield, *The Unheavenly City*, 2nd ed. (Boston: Little, Brown, 1974).
35. James Fallows, "The Passionless Presidency," *The Atlantic*, 243 (May 1979).
36. This is over and above other costs of spontaneity in terms of poor decisions about what to seek in the first place.
37. John Locke, *Second Treatise on Civil Government* (Eerdmans Publishing Company: Grand Rapids, 1978), pp. 33–34.
38. "Cronkite Sues Over Store's Use of Name," in "Notes on People," *New York Times*, November 17, 1978.
39. Richard E. Cohen, "SALT II—Selling the Treaty to the Senate," *National Journal* 11, June 16, 1979.
40. Durkheim, Emile, *The Elementary Forms of Religious Life* (New York: Macmillan, 1915).
41. In the language of economics, one may conceptualize what is being done here as raising the price obtainable for something by means of product differentiation. (The price is raised because exchanging something only for other things within its sphere requires a person to "pay" for the thing in one particular kind of production, rather than allowing him to pay through another kind of production that he might be better at.) The negative implication of the use of product differentiation to raise price arises, however, from the suspicion that the demand for the differentiated features of the product is partly induced by the producer. In these cases, however, demand often comes spontaneously from the "buyer."
42. It might be objected that the person who regrets an exchange made in a moment of weakness could always buy back the thing with the money (or whatever) he just got for it. This is sometimes possible, but not in cases where an action at the moment of succumbing to temptation has implications

for some later period—as in signing a contract or suffering long-term health damage. The costs of the act of succumbing to temptation are also not reversible.

43. The pangs felt should be distinguished from information-gathering costs in decision making, which do fit neatly into economic models. These costs may make some exchanges unworthwhile that would have been worthwhile had the costs not existed. But nobody would ever blanch at having an exchange offered him where the expected information costs would be too great to make the exchange worthwhile. He would simply say, "No thank you, but it's going to cost me too much to gather the information to find out whether this is worthwhile." Pangs, however, are felt as soon as the offer is contemplated.

44. On these points, see Albert O. Hirschman, *The Passions and the Interests: Arguments for Capitalism Before Its Triumph* (Princeton: Princeton University Press, 1977).

45. Durkheim, *Division of Labor*, op cit.

46. See, for instance, Philip Kotler, *Marketing Management*, 3rd edition (Englewood Cliffs: Prentice-Hall, 1976), Ch. 1–3.

47. It might be argued that one could deal with these external effects as with external effects in general, not by banning the behavior in question—in this case market exchange—but by Coasian bribes or by taxes. One could thus pay someone not to place something on the market. The problem with such an approach is obvious; it would require somebody who desired to reduce the scope of the market to use market mechanisms to get the scope reduced, thus defeating the original purpose of his intervention.

48. Edith Stokey and Richard Zeckhauser, *A Primer for Policy Analysis* (New York: Norton, 1978), pp. 292–93.

49. Charles Frankel makes a similar point in "The Rights of Nature," in Lawrence H. Tribe et al., (eds), *When Values Conflict* (Cambridge: Ballinger, 1976), p. 104.

50. "Entrepreneurs Cash in on Airlines' Half-Fare Coupons," *New York Times*, June 7, 1979.

51. For an expansion of these themes on free choice, see Steven Kelman, "Regulation and Paternalism," *Public Policy*, 29 (Spring 1981).

Chapter 3

ECONOMIC INCENTIVES AND ENVIRONMENTAL POLICY: REACTIONS OF POLICY PARTICIPANTS

In this chapter, the focus of our inquiry shifts gear. Up to this point, I have presented a normative critique of the case for the use of economic incentives in environmental policy. Here I present the empirical results of a survey of participants in the environmental policy-making process, conducted by two research assistants and me in the winter of 1978, to assess knowledge about and opinions of proposals to move from using standards in environmental policy to using charges.

The initial research out of which this book has grown was undertaken by economists interested in thinking through the details of implementation of economic incentive approaches to specific areas of environmental regulation. They imported in (so to speak) a political scientist—myself—to help answer why economic incentive approaches to environmental regulation, despite their long advocacy by economists, had made so little headway in the political system. Hence the origin of the interviews reported on in this chapter. As will be discussed in the next chapter, in the period since the survey was conducted, economic incentive approaches in fact began to make some headway within EPA, although not in the form that economists traditionally advocated them. While economic incentive approaches seem thus to have ended their long wandering in the desert, the interview results remain valuable despite these changes, because they reveal the values and conceptions that various participants in environmental policy making bring to debates about economic incentive proposals.

The Survey

The criteria for selecting respondents for the survey were simple. Selected were: (1) every staff member (Democratic and Republican) of the Subcommittee on the Environment of the Senate Environment and Public Works Committee, the Subcommittee on Water Resources of the House Public Works and Transportation Committee, and the Subcommittee on Health of the House Interstate and Foreign Commerce Committee; (2) the personal staffs of the members of the relevant committees who reported spending a "significant" amount of their time on environmental policy (not all the House subcommittee members had personal staffs who devoted any significant time to environmental policy); and (3) all the professional staff of the Washington offices of environmentalist organizations and trade associations (identified in a publication provided by the EPA public affairs office) who dealt with air and water pollution, and, for environmental groups, solid waste as well. No executive branch officials, either in the White House or the EPA, were interviewed. We sent letters explaining the project and called to arrange interviews. In order not to bias replies, respondents were not informed in advance of the specific interest the researchers had in attitudes towards economic incentive approaches. Nobody refused to see us. The total number of respondents was sixty-three. This number is too small to make possible any sophisticated analysis of the data, especially when it is divided up by respondent group. The data will therefore be displayed as simple marginals or, occasionally, in twofold crosstabulations.

The interviews generally lasted between forty-five minutes and two hours. Almost every question was of a fixed-format, open-ended type, and responses have been classified into various categories for the purposes of the tables to follow. (The text of the survey instrument appears in the Appendix.) A number of broad, open-ended interviews were done before the final questionnaire was developed in order to get a sense of what kinds of themes people brought up. Due to the length of the interviews and the differing amounts of time that different respondents had free in which to talk, in most cases not every question was asked of every respondent. There was no tendency, however, for the more "important" respondents to give us less time than other respondents; if anything, the opposite may have been the case. The marginals and crosstabulations to be presented, therefore, often are based on a subset of those interviewed.

Questions in the first third of the interview dealt with the respondent's background, solicited information about the respondent's major criticisms of existing environmental policy, and asked about information sources the respondents had for new ideas. These questions were asked before any of the specific questions on economic incentives. The idea was to see what concerns respondents expressed spontaneously, before the subject of the interview turned to charges.

Survey Results: Overall

The results of the interviews in many ways were startling. One initial hypothesis had been that if economic incentive proposals had not gotten further, this might in significant measure have been because such proposals raised implementation problems which academic economists were not likely to have considered. Many ideas that seem attractive end up being much less so because their implementation would require organizational capabilities that cannot be created. The assumption was that people closer to the day-to-day formulation of environmental policy would provide information on the "boring details" that so often stand between the grand visions of those conceiving new policy ideas and the real world outcomes desired. In fact, however, respondents did not supply any new reasons, garnered from their greater practical experience, to reject charges proposals as theoretically appealing but organizationally unachievable.

What the interviews did hint at, instead, was just how much proposals to use economic incentives for environmental policy did raise the very issues that were discussed in the preceding chapter—issues about what kind of society we want to live in. I believe therefore that these kinds of concerns do indeed help crucially in explaining controversy over proposals to use economic incentives. I want to emphasize that in significant measure the line of reasoning developed in the preceding chapter emerged in response to the kinds of answers we were getting in the inteviews. It developed as I attempted to think through points that were being raised at a fairly intuitive level by our respondents; these points did not seem to "mesh" with the organizing principles that economists advocating charges were using to look at the world. I hope that my report of the responses we got from our respondents is not significantly influenced by my overall conclusion that the concerns about what kind of society we would be creating by using economic incentives in environmental policy are very important in understanding why the use of economic incentives met with resistance when proposed. I do not believe this is the case.

The interviews showed that economic incentive approaches did have supporters among participants in environmental policy making, most strongly among Republican congressional staff. But these supporters did not, by and large, support charges because of their efficiency advantages. Indeed *the interviews showed surprisingly little knowledge of the nature of—or even the existence of—the efficiency argument for charges*. Advocates supported charges in significant measure because of a general conviction in favor of markets and against "government interference." Opponents of charges also tended to be unfamiliar with the efficiency arguments. Those environmentalists (and their congressional allies) who were opposed to charges were partly worried about the strategic effect on the political prospects for maintaining strong environmental laws of moving from standards to charges. They were concerned about the effect of moving jurisdiction over environmental issues from congressional environmental committees, with many committed environmentalist members, to tax-writing committees, regarded as more conservative and less proenvironment. They also showed worry about the effect of reopening environmental laws to the revision that would be required to set up a charges system at a time when environmentalists were politically not as strong as they had been when the original legislation was passed in 1970 and 1972. But for many environmentalists and their congressional allies, a key element in their reaction to charges proposals was, just as for supporters, their general ideological or philosophical attitude towards the market and towards government.

Table 3-1   Attitudes Toward Charges (entire sample)

For	23%
Against	57%
For experiments (in areas currently unregulated, in one region) but against full implementation	17%
For, but only with very gradual implementation	2%
For a hybrid system of charges and standards	2%
	(N = 61)

(Percentages add up to greater than 100% because of rounding.)

The survey showed that nearly every respondent had heard of proposals to use charges in environmental policy; only 2 of 63 respondents had not. (They were both personal staff of congressional environmental committee members.) Furthermore, virtually all respondents, in answer to the question "Could you explain why some people regard charges as superior to standards?" were able to cite some arguments that proponents of charges make. And the responses showed that support for a charges approach was not insignificant. Table 3-1 displays responses for the sample as a whole as to whether they favored introducing charges to replace regulation that uses standards.

Two things immediately stand out in the survey responses taken as a whole. The first is the pattern of support and opposition to economic incentive approaches. The most sympathetic group was Republican committee staff. Of the four members of the Republican staff of the Subcommittee on the Environment of the Senate Public Works Committee, three supported moving to a charges approach. All three, in fact, *spontaneously* mentioned failure to use economic incentives in their responses to the questions on criticisms of previous environmental policy and/or new approaches to environmental policy. The most united opponents of charges were members of the Democratic committee staff. The five Democratic counterparts to the Senate Republican committee staff were *all* opposed to economic incentive approaches. (Interestingly, the one Republican Senate staff member interviewed who opposed charges said he was a Democrat when hired to work for a Republican senator on the committee; he decided to go to Washington on the recommendation of a professor in the environmental law program where he was studying, and the job with this Republican senator, from whose home state he came, was the best one available when he looked.) Environmentalists interviewed, by contrast, were split. Thirty-two percent were classified as favoring charges, 16% as favoring experimenting with them on a limited basis to see how they worked, while 37% were hostile (N = 19). Industry environmental lobbyists were mostly opposed to charges—15% were classified as favoring them while 85% were opposed (N = 20).

The pattern of responses above—with the exception perhaps of the industry hostility—appears to suggest a liberal-conservative ideological tenor to the reactions of respondents. This impression is dramatically confirmed by an examination of answers to the question where respondents were asked to cite arguments that economic incentives proponents made in favor of charges. What stands out dramatically was how few respondents in *any* of the groups surveyed cited the efficiency argument for charges. In the sample taken as a whole, only 16% spontaneously cited the efficiency argument as among the arguments charge proponents make for their proposals. (To be counted as having cited the argument, the respondent need not have used the word "efficiency," but only have explained in a minimally sufficient way the idea of cost minimization in achieving a certain goal.)

Respondents who did not spontaneously mention the efficiency argument for charges were specifically asked two follow-up questions. The first was: "The argument is sometimes made that using charges we could obtain any given degree of environmental quality for a lower cost than by using standards. Have you ever heard this argument for charges?" Sixty-four percent of the respondents who had not spontaneously mentioned the efficiency argument earlier (N = 36) claimed to have heard the argument. Yet, when then asked a follow-up, "Could you explain on what basis people make this argument?" *not a single one* was able to do so. Fifty-five percent (N = 43) could give no explanation at all, and 44% gave arguments that related to a general ideological case for charges ("Costs less because less bureaucracy costs less," or "Costs less because the regulated parties have more information and experience than the regulators"). A few of those who were unable to explain the efficiency argument, although not a large number, made reference to having seen arguments economists made in support of the contention, but added frankly that they were unable to understand the argument. ("I've seen graphs and crossing dia-grams." "Lots of economists talk a lot of gobbledygook that the average layman can't understand.") Respondents were also asked, in the section of the survey that preceded the explicit question on charges, "If you think of different sources of a given type of pollutant, is it your impression that different sources tend to face relatively similar costs in attaining any given proportion of pol-lution abatement or very different costs?" A large majority of respondents were aware that different sources often faced very different costs—a key factual component of the efficiency argument for charges. (The percentage was 89%, N = 45, for all respond-ents, with no difference between industry and nonindustry re-spondents.) Yet only 2 of the 24 respondents asked mentioned charges in answering the follow-up question, "How would you go about dealing with this problem of differing costs?" Thus, although the survey showed economic incentive proposals most definitely had advocates, the efficiency argument in support of such pro-posals appeared to have passed most respondents by. This finding is especially surprising considering that those interviewed were people who spend all their time thinking and learning about en-vironmental issues, and that economists had been persistently writing on the theme of the efficiency advantages of charges for a decade. Furthermore, the lack of knowledge about the efficiency argument for charges stood out especially in the context of general awareness of the fact that there existed people who thought charges were a good idea and who made arguments for them. It wasn't that our respondents didn't think there were arguments for charges, it is only that the efficiency argument, for most of them, was not one of them.[1]

The arguments that had made the most impression on respond-ents (with the exception of those in industry, to whom I will return shortly) were those best described as ideological or philosophical. Proponents of charges were endorsing, in a general ideological way, "the market" and excoriating government and bureaucrats; opponents of charges were uneasy about or hostile to "the market" and more convinced of the necessity of a government role, bu-reaucrats and all.

Survey Responses of Congressional Staff

The tendency to give ideological responses appeared most clearly in the responses of the congressional environmental committee staffers, particularly the Senate Democratic and Republican staffers. Table 3-2 displays the number of respondents who mentioned different arguments for charges in response to a question about what arguments supporters of charges made in support of such proposals. (There were only five Democratic senator staffers on the Subcommittee and four Republican staffers. Percentages should therefore be interpreted accordingly. Also, percentages add up to greater than 100% because respondents could mention more than one argument.) Table 3-3 displays responses to the follow-up question, "In your *own* view, what are some of the disadvantages, if any, of charges as over standards?"

Democratic Senate subcommittee staffers were hostile to charges, while Republican Senate subcommittee staffers were enthusiastic. When asked to recite what arguments were generally made in favor of charges, *both* groups emphasized general ideological arguments ("less bureaucracy," "uses the market," "appeals to self-interest"). When asked to cite what they themselves saw as the

Table 3-2 Senate Committee Staffer Arguments Cited for Charges

Argument	Percentage of Respondents Who Cited Argument	
	Senate Democratic	*Senate Republican*
Charges made it in one's self-interest to reduce pollution	60%	25%
Ease of enforcement	60	0
Less bureaucracy; simplicity	40	100
Promarket or antigovernment comment without further justification; general "prochoice" comment	20	75
Correctly stated efficiency argument	20	25
Stated efficiency argument but did not understand it well	20	0
Incentive to go beyond a standard	20	25
Internalized costs, "polluters should pay"	20	25
"Based on cost-benefit considerations"	20	0
Encourage technical innovation	0	25
	(N = 5)	(N = 4)

Table 3-3   What Respondents Saw as Disadvantages of Charges (Senate Committee Staff)

Argument	Percentage of Respondents Who Made Argument	
	Senate Democratic	*Senate Republican*
One should not have a choice of polluting, if willing to pay a charge; "license to pollute"	80%	25%
Health damage should never be allowed; one cannot set a monetary value on health or the environment	80	0
Political environment now is less in favor of environmental controls; reopening the issue risks ending up with looser standards	40	0
Politically difficult to set the charges high enough	20	0
Administrative problems; difficult to monitor, too much bureaucracy	20	25
High cost of changing from the present system, given that system is in place	20	25
Industry could just pass on costs and not control pollution	20	0
Charges difficult to set; technical and economic information needed	0	100
Results are uncertain	0	25
Inequitable (would not allow variances); would hit the poor companies too hard; would concentrate industry	0	25

disadvantages of charges, the hostile Democratic Senate subcommittee staffers also tended to give ideological objections: "shouldn't have a choice to pay and pollute," "license to pollute," "can't put a monetary price on health or the environment." Some Democratic staffers were also worried about the political difficulties of setting charges high enough, particularly at a time of less interest in the environment than when environmental legislation was passed. By contrast, the main problem the Republican staffers mentioned was the technical difficulty of setting charge levels—a narrowly focused, nonideological concern that not a single Senate Democratic subcommittee staffer mentioned.

The most important figure in the formulation of environmental policy in the United States in the 1970s was Senator Edmund

Muskie, then Chairman of the Subcommittee on the Environment. The major occasion when Muskie spoke publicly on charge proposals was in a Senate floor debate in November 1971 with Senator William Proxmire, who had introduced an amendment for using effluent charges to pending clean water legislation. (Proxmire in turn was influenced by environmental economists on his staff.)

In the Senate floor debate in 1971 Muskie stated that, "We cannot give anyone the option of polluting for a fee."[2] Proxmire, in his procharge arguments on the floor, never presented the efficiency argument for charges. Instead, he argued that charges would be more easily enforced with less bureaucracy. Muskie counterargued that charges would not require less bureaucracy than standards. The debate included frequent references from both sides to "the cost of cleaning up," as if that cost were constant across different pollution sources. And when the subject of charges again came up in a Senate hearing in 1977, with Senator Gary Hart discussing economic incentives favorably and emphasizing that it would be less bureaucratic, Muskie again rejected the notion that charges would involve less bureaucracy.

The two most important Democratic staff people in Congress who were dealing with the environment at the time of the survey were Karl Braithwaite and Leon Billings. At the time of the interviews, Braithwaite had recently become director of the subcommittee's professional staff. Before coming to the committee in the early 1970's, he had been a political science professor who had taught environmental policy. Billings had worked for Subcommittee Chairman Muskie since the mid-1960s and was majority staff director when air and water legislation was written in the early 1970s.

In a brief interview, Billings began by stating that "there is a basic philosophical difference between regulatory people and economists. Economists don't care whether you achieve a reduction of pollution. *They* don't really care, but *we* really do care. The economic approach is inequitable, because it permits a choice on the part of the polluter whether to spend on pollution control or on other things." Billings went on to say that the problem with economists was that "they worship things economic." Billings stated that he had "heard" the efficiency argument and added that "it may or may not be valid." He was not able to explain it.

Instead, he used the question to express distaste for economists, whom he regarded as "zealots."

Braithwaite gave a lengthy interview that mixed strategic with philosophical opposition to charges. "The biggest argument the proponent of charges made is that you get an automatic correctiveness by drawing in more market forces. They love the market, and they want to readjust the equation slightly for externalities so that the market can go ahead and run." He said another main argument for charges was that they embodied a cost-benefit approach, "since you're never justified in setting the charge at more than what cost-benefit analysis tells you is justified." He continued,

All we ever hear about from industry is about costs. Our members, though, listen to people talking about values they want to protect— nature and parks and health. We had a guy who testified here who was ultrasensitive to pollution. The committee has to decide whether we want to protect a guy like this. How do you quantify that?

Braithwaite went on to say that using charges to deal with solid waste was more acceptable than for air and water "because there is nothing that hurts your health about an excessive candy bar wrapper." Finally, Braithwaite also rebutted the argument, which he thought was an important part of the case for charges, that they would mean less bureaucracy. And his last words in the interview were, "The fact that industry is opposed to this is one of the best points in its favor. Maybe if EPA gets captured we'll need this. But that's not the case now."

Quotes from the interviews with the other three Democratic staffers give a flavor of their concerns:

The best argument they make is that industry works on the basis of the profit motive and that they will respond best to a pollution control system which uses the same motive. The philosophical assumption that proponents of charges make is that there is a free market system that responds to pressures and that responds to relative costs. I reject that assumption. I grew up with Lockheed loans and auto emission price fixing and cost passions.

The argument for pollution charges is that since we do have a capitalist framework, an economic driving force is more effective. . . . But I'm troubled by the psychology of it. If there's a national program, that says we want every corporation to become part of achieving that goal. To allow them to buy their way out is not good national psychology. It's like buying your way out of the army. If

*you're rich enough to pay a gas guzzler tax, you can buy your way
out of our national policy.*

*The things I want to attain with environmental policy aren't
quantifiable. These values can't be preserved if the calculation is
essentially a business calculation. . . . The people I have spoken
with about charges were mostly academicians. They struck me as
being ignorant of environmental values. I can't imagine writing off
300,000 people in Los Angeles. I don't know how much I'd be willing
to pay, but it's lots more than we're talking about. The Clean Air
Act was written to protect vulnerable segments of the population.
(By contrast) I'd be more willing to see a charge approach for solid
wastes. There's an economic value there in helping cities save money
in managing solid wastes, and that's more compatible with an economic approach than in the case of air and water.*

What was perhaps most striking about the arguments of the
Republican staffers was the failure of two of three supporters of
economic incentives to present the efficiency argument for charges.
The senior Republican staff member for the subcommittee stated
spontaneously early in the interview that "philosophically, the
market mechanism has greater appeal" than regulatory approaches. When asked about arguments proponents made in favor
of charges, he did correctly state the efficiency argument, but only
after stating that the first argument for charges was that it would
"get decisions made by the guy who's going to pay rather than
by the bureaucracy." After discussing problems he saw with getting charge proposals through Congress and setting charge levels,
he concluded that on balance he was for using charges "because
I trust the marketplace more than the bureaucracy."

Two other minority subcommittee staff members were more
enthusiastic—and also more ideological. Both spontaneously mentioned economic incentives early on in the interview; neither saw
any significant drawbacks to charges. But both thought that
charges would be cheaper than standards only because the bureaucracy would be taken out of things. "Charges will be cheaper
for a similar level of control, because there would be less administrative cost," said one. "You could get a whole lot better working
out in the market, without bureaucratic enforcement," said the
other. "Things take place independent of a big structure." As for
the arguments for charges, it was first mentioned that it "relies
on market mechanisms rather than bureaucrats having to make
judgments. Market forces made the determination instead." Both
respondents gave similar responses when asked who the main

opponents of charge proposals would be. "People who like government meddling," was one response. "People disenchanted with the marketplace and private enterprise" was the other. The current regulation strategy had come about because of "disenchantment with the marketplace and private enterprise" and "a desire to kick industry in the ass."

Of the other congressional staffers, those whose responses were most similar to their Senate subcommittee counterparts were Democratic staffers for the Subcommittee on Health of the House Interstate and Foreign Commerce Committee. (This subcommittee had no Republican staff.) The Interstate and Foreign Commerce Committee is the site of a great many ideological battles (over health care issues, notably, as well as air pollution). The chief staffer on air pollution for the House subcommittee expressed an ambivalence towards charges that, he stated, expressed his ambivalence about what attitude to take towards "bad" behavior such as that of polluters. He was afraid that charges "might relegate social policy decisions to the polluters." Health, he continued, "is a moral issue, and I'm afraid of putting the fox in charge of the chicken coop by leaving this to the judgment of the private sector." Asked later in the interview whether, if a charge were put on driving a car into downtown that reflected the social costs such driving imposes, he would still criticize somebody who drove his car and paid the charge rather than taking available public transportation, the staffer replied:

> *I have mixed feelings. It has to do with my own personal political migration. It used to be that I would have criticized such a person harshly. Now I have some sympathy for allowing him the freedom to do what he wants. But my migration isn't complete. There's still something within me that wants people to do the right thing.*

By contrast, the House Committee on Public Works and Transportation is traditionally a fairly conservative, southern-dominated committee that oversees many "pork barrel" projects in addition to its jurisdiction over water pollution legislation. The staff on that committee, both Democratic and Republican, appeared to be somewhat less ideological, and concerned about charges as much for their potential to disrupt the program as for any other reason.

The personal staffs of senators who were members of the subcommittee, and even more so the personal staffs for House members (who must subdivide their time among many more issues), were generally much less knowledgeable than the committee staffs about charges. It was in this group of ten that the only two respondents who had never heard of charges proposals were found.

At the time the interviews were conducted, there was one self-proclaimed advocate of charges among the actual senators and congressmen who sat on these committees. This was Gary Hart, a first-term senator from Colorado. During the 1977 hearings on revisions of the Clean Water Act, Hart frequently asked witnesses questions about their attitudes to charge proposals. That same year he also proposed using a tax on nitrogen oxide auto emissions as a way of breaking the deadlock between the auto industry and environmentalists on whether to relax auto emissions standards written into the Clean Air Act amendments of 1970.

Key in this context was the apparent reason for Hart's stand. A product of the antiwar protest movement of the 1960s, Hart managed George McGovern's presidential campaign in 1972. The "new politics" movement out of which Hart emerged initially differed from traditional American liberalism in its relative skepticism about the benevolence of government, a skepticism nurtured by anti-Vietnam involvement, and a greater relative concern for "quality of life" as opposed to New Deal welfare state issues. In the political climate of the 1970s, such concern became translated into attempts to develop a new political approach that mixed "liberal" concern with issues such as the environment or pursuit of unconventional lifestyles with "conservative" hostility to government intervention in people's lives. Hart, who was once quoted as stating that the new generation of liberals didn't want to be "little Hubert Humphreys," became one of the spearheads among younger members of Congress of this new amalgam.

Advocacy of economic incentive proposals for environmental policy fit exquisitely into this vision, and Hart embraced such advocacy warmly as soon as the notion was presented to him. But, again, the reasons had much more to do with general ideological concerns than with efficiency. Hart presented his views at a Senate hearing with EPA Administrator Russell Train.[3]

> *I see the country approaching . . . what I consider to be a small crisis in our government's entire regulatory approach to human conduct. . . . [W]e must begin to think very seriously about substituting for this regulatory approach the economic incentive approach. It is not foolproof. It is not perfect. But the time is rapidly*

*approaching when the citizens of this country are just going to
routinely toss out of office people who continue to support more
regulation in their life. . . . It is stifling people's freedom.*

One of Hart's two environmental aides was able to state correctly
the efficiency argument for charges, while the other was not. Both,
however, emphasized other things. The "politically sexy side" of
charge proposals, one of the aides stated in an interview, was that
"political demagogues are getting elected on the basis of less
government interference with your lives." Charges were a way
to have your environmental cake and still be able to answer those
concerns about governmental interference. Charges would encourage polluters to lower pollution levels even below those set
by standards. Using charges, the aide continued, "we may be able
to get a better level of environmental quality that would be politically infeasible with standards. Complying with the standards
isn't enough. We want to get lower than that." And charges would
allow people to decide for themselves. "If you can get better
results than the existing approach and get the government off your
back, you have a winner," the aide concluded. In response to a
later question on parking bans versus transportation surcharges,
the same aide responded that he favored surcharges over bans
because "with a fee, a person makes a decision himself. People
ought to make decisions themselves. They're happy when they
do." He continued, "A charge allows more options. Parking bans
allow fewer options."

Survey Responses of Environmentalists

As a group, environmentalists were by far the most knowledgeable
about charges—and also the most split. Table 3-4 shows the arguments cited by environmentalists for charges. Thirty-two percent cited the efficiency arguments—not an overwhelming percentage, but impressive compared to the 0% of industrial
respondents and 10% of the congressional staffers. Table 3-5 shows
the disadvantages environmentalists saw.

With the exception of the relatively frequent mention of the
efficiency argument and the "internalize costs" argument, the arguments that environmentalists cited in favor of charges were
relatively similar to those cited by Senate staffers. So were the

Table 3-4   Environmentalist Arguments Made for Charges

Argument	Percentage of Respondents Who Made Arguments
Correctly stated efficiency argument	32%
Charges make it in one's self-interest to reduce pollution	32
Internalize costs; "polluters should pay"	32
Less bureaucracy, simplicity	25
Ease of enforcement	16
Knew no arguments	16
Promarket or antigovernment comment without further justification, general "prochoice" comment	11
Incentive to go beyond a standard	5
Uniformity	5
"Based on cost-benefit considerations"	5
Gives arguments for noncompliance fee only	5
	(N = 19)

Table 3-5   What Environmentalists Saw as Disadvantages of Charges

Argument	Percentage of Respondents Who Made Argument
One should not have a choice of polluting if willing to pay a charge; "license to pollute"	37%
Health damage should never be allowed; one cannot set a monetary value on health or the environment	37
Politically difficult to set the charges high enough	26
Charges difficult to set; technical and economic information needed	16
Results are uncertain	16
Difficulty in going from ambient health response to emissions charge	16
High cost of changing from the present system	11
Industry could just pass on costs and not control pollution	11
Inequitable (would not allow variances); would hit the poor companies too hard; would concentrate industry	11
Political climate now is less in favor of environmental controls; reopening the issue risks ending up with looser standards	5
Industry uncertainty	5
	(N = 19)

disadvantages they saw. In other words, there was a significant element of general philosophy or ideology.

In explaining their views further, respondents who were worried about charges on ideological or philosophical grounds tended to express their views in rather intuitive terms. This is hardly surprising, since respondents were trained neither as philosophers nor economists. Yet strands of concerns about the necessity to stigmatize polluting behavior, about the psychological costs of markets, and about equity considerations in policy design all emerged.

The issue of stigmatizing polluting behavior came up in the context of concerns about charges being a "license to pollute" and in discussions of using words such as "criminal" and "blame" in relation to the behavior of polluters.

Tied for the most frequently expressed concern about economic incentives was that they would grant an unacceptable "license to pollute." Thirty-seven percent of environmentalist respondents mentioned the "license to pollute" argument. And those mentioning these arguments were also more likely to oppose charges (see Table 3-6).

Some of the Democratic staffers and environmentalists who raised the "license to pollute" argument appeared indeed to be mainly worried—as the response economists make to the "license to pollute" contention suggests—about whether the level of the charge would be set high enough to decrease polluting behavior significantly. And it may well be that some staffers or environmentalists were in fact ignorant of the economic insight that raising the price of a behavior means that less of it is done.

But most of the unease about charges being a "license to pollute"

Table 3-6 **Support for Charges Among Environmentalists and Senate Majority Staff by Mentioning of Various Disadvantages**

	For	*Against*	*For Experiments, but Against Full Implementation*	
Mentioned "can't set price" argument	14%	71%	14%	(N = 7)
Mentioned "license to pollute" argument	17	33	50	(N = 7)
Mentioned neither argument	50	38	12	(N = 8)

seemed to reflect concerns that are not addressed simply by arguing that the level of the charge can be made higher. This is illustrated by comments such as:

> *The demand for charges reflects the deep resentment people had at being called criminals. They want to put this on a businesslike basis. But I'm not ready to abandon that approach.*

> *When you have a manipulative approach like this, it isn't a societally stated goal to clean up rivers.*

> *I think there's something anomalous about taxing poison. A tax appears to sanction the poisoning.*

> *How many people would feel that by paying their money they're absolved of guilt?*

> *People should not pollute. The decision should not be up to them.*

> *I don't like the idea that pollution is a matter of choice. You shouldn't be able to pay for it.*

> *A guy living in the suburbs, driving a big car, using luxury appliances, should be blamed. It is morally wrong. There are alternatives. People can use carpools. People don't need electric can openers. There's a clear moral issue there.*

> *I don't think anyone has the right to go out and ruin our environment.*

> *Nader uses the term "environmental violence." I think he has a point.*

> *One day a courageous district attorney will prosecute these people for murder.*

Two questions were asked to explore judgmental attitudes by environmentalists. They were:

> *Let's say that a parking surcharge, developed as part of a transportation control program, reflected the costs a driver imposes on society by driving a car, including the damages from auto pollution. If the surcharge reflected all such costs, would you then feel it was OK for a person to drive his car in the city center as long as he paid the surcharge, or would you still criticize him for not taking available public transportation?*

> *Let's say that a charge is added onto packaging materials which reflects the damage that such materials cause society—including both the costs of disposal and the aesthetic damage litter causes. If such a charge reflected all the damage, would you then feel that if a consumer wishes to buy the packaging and pay the extra costs, it's OK for him to do so, or would you still criticize such a consumer for being wasteful?*

Sixty-seven percent of the environmentalists ($N = 12$) said they would still criticize the car driver; even 40% ($N = 10$) would criticize the package buyer, though many respondents specifically stated that solid waste involved less of a "moral issue" than air and water pollution because of the absence of health effects. This attitude appeared repeatedly during deliberations in 1977 and 1978 within the interagency Resource Conservation Committee. This committee had been set up under a provision of the 1976 Resource Recovery and Conservation Act to investigate the possibility of introducing a national product charge for packaging material such as paper. Some studies done for the committee estimated that the addition to the price of packaging material of a charge reflecting its solid waste cleanup costs would reduce consumption of such material only insignificantly. Most economists would react to this finding by stating that addition of the charge would mean that packaging consumers were bearing the social cost of their behavior and that, given this, the quantity of packaging then consumed is a matter of indifference. Yet the virtually universal reaction of those considering product charges was very different: the studies played an important role in diminishing enthusiasm for the product charge, because "they showed that product charges won't work." By "won't work" was meant that they wouldn't reduce packaging consumption sufficiently. The initial assumption was that "excessive" consumption of packaging was wrong. A product charge would be accepted if it achieved a significant reduction in consumption; that it made packaging reflect its social cost, without significant consumption effects, was regarded as unimpressive.

During the 1970 House hearings on air pollution legislation, the following dialogue took place between Congressman David Satterfield and Dennis Hayes, head of Environmental Action:[4]

> *Mr. Satterfield:* I was interested to note when you started off that you mentioned something about this being a time we hear about law and order and then referring to "industrial criminals."
>
> I am interested in the use of this word. We hear more and more about "industrial criminals." Actually, you don't have any criminals in this country unless there is a law which is violated. Isn't that right?
>
> *Mr. Hayes:* Well, if you want to carry on a sort of semantic struggle, we are breaking a whole series of nature's laws.
>
> *Mr. Satterfield:* Don't you think you ought to state this is the type of criminality you are talking about rather than making a

blanket statement that we have a lot of industrial criminals in this country?

Mr. Hayes: Mr. Congressman, there are a whole series of things that are being done in industries that are fairly well documented right now which are contributing enormously to the degradation of the world, and probably in an irreversible manner. That kind of action, whether or not this body or a state legislature has seen fit to pass a law, is criminal. As I was using the term, a criminal is a person or institution who robs others of their rights to an ecologically balanced world.

In response to an early question in the survey on what criticisms they would make of recent environmental policy, 22% of environmentalists and Senate Democratic staffers (N = 23) spontaneously mentioned a response coded as "low popular environmental consciousness." The frequency of this response takes on added meaning as an indication of the topic's importance, since the question referred to "environmental policy" and thus would appear to summon forth responses about government policy rather than individual preferences. Environmentalists are concerned about the battle for preferences and about social statements of stigmatization of polluting behavior.

Environmentalists and congressional staffers were also asked a question designed to tap their attitudes towards using the morally condemnatory word "criminal" to describe the behavior of polluters. The question read:

> *Would you personally ever use the word "criminal" to describe the behavior of some individual or company which pollutes the environment? (If yes) Under what circumstances?*

This question helped measure whether respondents took an attitude of condemnation towards polluters. The coders classified 76% of respondents (N = 21) as having a basically positive attitude towards the use of the word "criminal" to describe the behavior of many polluters. Furthermore, although the results should be interpreted with caution because of the small size of the survey and the small number of respondents who looked unfavorably on the use of the word "criminal," there was a definite tendency for those who reacted favorably towards the use of the word "criminal" to be more hostile towards charges than those who reacted positively (Table 3-7). Even more dramatically, of respondents to that question who used the word in a legal sense only (and explicitly excluded a broader usage), 75% favored charges, while of the

Table 3-7 Attitudes Toward Use of the Word "Criminal" vis-à-vis Attitudes Toward Charges (Environmentalists and Senate Democratic Staffers)

	Attitude to Charges		
	For	*Against*	*For Experiments, but Against Full Implementation*
Favorable to use of the word "criminal"	25%	44%	19%
Unfavorable to use of the word "criminal"	50	25	25
		(N = 20)	

respondents who used it in a more inclusive sense (including "polluting knowingly"), not a single one favored charges (N = 10). There were similar results for the question, "Do you think it is useful to use the word 'blame' in reference to responsibility for pollution, or do you think that this is not a useful word?" Although environmentalists and majority staffers were more split on their attitude to the word (58% coded as favorable), those who were positive were more likely to oppose charges than those who weren't.

Some statements on the use of the word "criminal" by environmentalists or majority staffers who opposed charges were:

> That's a problem with the economic approach, that it doesn't distinguish between willful and nonwillful. Economists don't see that distinction. These words are important in environmental policy. A crime against nature is a crime against society. I am part of a policy that has been adopted and that has an important goal. If I violate that policy, that's the same as if I rape, pillage, and burn. Society should be vengeful and punitive against violators of this policy. If my son dies of cancer, I want to blame somebody, and I want that somebody to be accountable.

> I hold both the natural and the human environment on a pedestal. When a human knowingly is destroying the natural environment or the human environment of the rest of the public for his own economic gain, that is criminal.

> I would use the word "criminal" on lots of occasions—much more often than it's generally used. It's easy to use it in cases like Kepone. But I would also use it for any willful behavior—it's a crime against society to dump harmful materials in the air and water.

> *Breaking a pollution law is not comparable to breaking a traffic law. It is similar to crimes against persons.*
>
> *It is criminal when there is a knowing abdication of responsibility.*

Note the contrast between these statements and ones on the same subject by environmentalists and congressional staffers who favored charges:

> *I don't use words like that. Polluters were responding to a market situation. You can't blame them. It's the way the system is structured.*
>
> *I wouldn't use the word "criminal." I wouldn't even use the word "bad." It's not a case of good actors or bad actors. It's a question of price signals.*

The second strand of the concern of many Democratic staffers and environmentalists about charges as a "license to pollute" involved the equity-based worry that those who would pay the charge rather than reducing their polluting behavior would be those who could more easily afford to do so. Thus, not only would the use of charges rather than standards remove the social statement that pollution is wrong; it would also open the way to a situation where the rich would continue to pollute, while the poor, who could not afford to pay the charge, would be the ones who would bear the burden of efforts to reduce pollution.

> *There's always somebody who can pay the price and buy the right to pollute.*
>
> *That's morally bad—its' a bad example for our children.*
>
> *With a pollution charge you're telling people to whom that's pocket change to pass that money on to their customers. I don't think it's fair.*
>
> *Say GE could afford the tax to pollute the Hudson. Do you want to grant someone the right to pollute and cause environmental and health consequences?*

When the idea was mentioned of using parking surcharges to limit car use rather than direct parking restrictions, one respondent stated, "My gut reaction is very strong on this. I hate it. I think it's elitist. I hate it for energy policy also."

As noted earlier, to apply the equity argument to charges for air and water pollution involves an unambiguous logical error. Nevertheless, it does apply to some other areas where economic incentive approaches are advocated, as well as to areas such as energy pricing where economists have been active in the debate. Democratic staffers or environmentalists can be expected to have heard such arguments there and inappropriately transferred their concern with equity issues in using pricing strategies to this area of environmental policy.

The second element of the deeper belief system of which uneasiness about charges forms a part was a general uneasiness about the market. For starters, most people who think about pollution regard the existence of environmental degradation as a failure (or at least a shortcoming) of the market system. (On the other hand, economists who analyze the problem of pollution, as noted earlier, think about pollution in terms of a failure to develop markets.) Unease about markets for those to whom pollution is a major issue, is, then, hardly surprising.

The unease was largely intuitive and general. Some of it, I feel with a fair degree of confidence, arises from a view of the psychological cost of markets. Other parts of it relate to sources as diverse as conventional views about oligopolistic lack of competition and a dislike for money because of its association with self-interest and inequality. Not all of these sources of unease about "the market" relate directly to the use of economic incentives in environmental policy, to be sure. But what appears to occur is a case of the power of words; a penumbra of associations with the concept "the market" becomes associated with proposals to "use the market." Most people who worry about "the market" have not analyzed their intuitions to any great extent. If they hear the expression, "use the market," they are likely to react based on their general perception of what "the market" implies.

The issue of the psychological costs of markets came out most specifically when respondents stated as a disadvantage of charges the view coded under the category "one cannot set a monetary price on health or the environment." (This was tied with "license to pollute" as the most frequently mentioned objection to using charges, cited by 37% of environmentalist respondents.)

A number of respondents palled at the idea of placing an explicit monetary price on pollution and, hence, on environmental quality.

> *If you contaminate the environment, I don't see how you can pick a tax that is worthwhile.*

> *We should make a rule that rivers are treasures and not fair game.*

I'm not really fond of the economists' tendency to be technocrats.

You can always make it profitable to kill people.

How do you figure out a tax for contaminating my wife's breast milk?

Some further hint of the nature of the unarticulated thoughts came from the frequent observations that using a charges approach would make pollution seem less like a health issue and more a simple question of esthetics. Other hints came from the view that a charges approach was more acceptable for solid waste than for air. Unlike clean air and water, garbage (as well as recycled materials) is already in the price system.

That staffers on Capitol Hill saw the question of whether to use charges from a general political or ideological perspective is perhaps not so surprising given that they are part of a political institution and that few had an environmental background. It was, however, a surprise to learn that many of the environmentalist lobbyists had a general political background rather than a specifically environmental one. Environmentalists were asked early in the interview what it was that initially got them interested in environmental problems. The question was asked to see whether there was any difference in support for charges between those whose initial interest was health related and those whose interest was wilderness related. It turned out, however, that many (37%) of the environmental lobbyists came into the environmental movement through general political concerns. An equally large group had their interest initially awakened by an interest in wilderness or the outdoors, while 26% initially had health-related interests, and an equal percentage came to the job for nonvalues-related reasons ("just a job," "a good opportunity," etc.).

Those who came to the environmental movement out of broader political reasons were social activists of the 1960s who, like many of their generation, moved from civil rights to Vietnam to the environment. They were critical of many aspects of American society; environmental problems were examples of larger social problems.

Table 3-8 shows that the source of initial interest in the environment influenced dramatically the attitudes of environmentalists and Senate Democratic staffers on charges. It also influenced the tendency to cite ideological arguments against charges (Table 3-9).

Table 3-8 Support for Charges by Source of Initial Environmental Interest (Environmentalists and Senate Democratic Staffers)

	Charge Attitudes		
	For	*Against*	*For Experiments, but Against Full Implementation*
Public Interest	20%	80%	0
Health	20	60	0
"Just as a job"; personal reasons	50	25	25%
Outdoors, wildlife	17	17	66
		(N = 20)	

Table 3-9 Citing Ideological Disadvantages of Charges by Initial Source of Environmental Interest (Environmentalists and Democratic Staffers)

	Arguments	
Initial Interest	*"License to Pollute"*	*"Can't Set a Price"*
Public Interest	60%	80%
Health	60	20
Nonvalues-Oriented	50	25
Nature/Wildlife	16	33
	(N = 20)	

Support for charges was nonetheless far greater among environmentalist lobbyists than among Democratic staffers. Two explanations may be cited. One is that environmentalists were more likely to know the efficiency arguments for charges than were the Democratic staffers. A second is that there appeared to be a greater tendency among environmentalists than among Democratic staffers to feel ambiguous, rather than hostile, about harnessing self-interest. A fair number of environmentalist respondents expressed a great respect for the power of self-interest to motivate behavior at the same time that they feared exclusive reliance on it. "Unfortunately, you can't turn everyone into an environmentalist on principle," stated one environmentalist, sympathetic to charges, who went on to describe himself as a "latent capitalist." After stating a moral criticism of charges, another respondent added, "But I know that's an idealistic approach to things, and I've been around." Another expressed well the ambivalence many felt:

In the sixties, I was involved in a Union Carbide case. I thought it was environmental violence. I met a reporter from Business Week, *who told me it was just a matter of dollars and cents. At the time, I totally disagreed. Now I'm more sympathetic. But, still, there is also a question of ethics and manners. People don't keep clean just because of a knowledge of disease.*

Survey Responses of Industry

Representatives of trade associations who dealt with environmental matters were also interviewed as part of the survey. One might expect industry people to be sympathetic to charges because they embody a market approach and because they encourage cost-benefit thinking. But the trade association people interviewed were among the most critical towards charges. They were also, as a group, the least informed about charges proposals. Although all stated they had heard such proposals made, they were less able to give an account of the argument that proponents made than were the other groups. The industry people were able to cite a mean of 1.5 arguments proponents made for charges, compared with a mean of 1.8 arguments cited by environmentalists, 2.8 by Democratic staff, and 3.0 by Republican staff. (In many instances, the interviewers skipped asking the industry people many of the detailed questions about charges on the survey questionnaire, because it put them in the embarrassing position of having to answer "don't know" to a series of questions, or to guess at or invent responses.)

Two differences between the industry and the environmental people help explain why the former were less knowledgeable about charges. First, they had fewer sources of information about policy alternatives. Second, they were more likely to limit their concerns about environmental policy to the issue of the stringency of EPA regulations.

A question in the survey asked respondents whether any charge proponent had ever spoken with them to convince them that charges were a good idea. Sixty-three percent of environmentalists (N = 8) said someone had spoken with them and 100% of Congressional staffers (N = 9). Only 17% of industry respondents (N = 6) said anybody had even spoken with them.

In the precharges part of the interview respondents were given

Table 3-10   Sources of New Ideas for Various Respondents

	Percentage Saying They Had No Source	*Mean No. of Sources for Those Citing Sources*
Industry	43%	1.25
Environmentalist	25%	1.67

	Percentage Citing Academics as Source (of Those Citing Sources)	*Percentage Citing Constituents as Source (of Those Citing Sources)*
Industry	7%	57%
Environmentalist	19%	38%

the statement, "You sometimes hear that it is hard for people involved in the day-to-day formulation of policy to find the time to consider policy alternatives or policy approaches different from those which come up in day-to-day legislative or agency battles." They were then asked to mention sources they might have. Table 3-10 compares the sources cited by the four groups interviewed. Note the larger number of industry respondents citing no sources, the smaller mean number of sources cited by industry respondents, and the far greater tendency of industry respondents to get information from their constituency (member firms), rather than from other sources. These sources are unlikely to direct the interest of trade association people towards new policy proposals. Not only were industry respondents unusually dependent for their information on member firms, but they were unusually dependent on them for their views as well. Both industry and environmentalist respondents were asked if there were any group whose support for charges would make them change their opinion. Sixty percent of industry respondents (N = 10) mentioned their constituency (i.e., member firms), a category not mentioned by a single environmentalist.

Second, industry respondents seemed unusually singleminded in their focus on the issue of the stringency of environmental regulations. For all the groups interviewed, the question of what level of protection environmental regulation should require was a central one. But a fair number of the industry respondents, during the portions of the interview dealing with charges, kept trying to move the subject away from a discussion of charges and back towards complaints that EPA was imposing unreasonable cleanup demands on industry.

Together, these circumstances suggest a picture of trade association lobbyists in a defensive posture, not so concerned with new ideas or policy alternatives as with warding off encroachments, and too dependent on member firms to take policy initiatives in these areas. Indeed, a number of industry respondents stated as much—that industry mainly tended to react to the proposals of others. They didn't think up new proposals themselves (and they probably wished that others wouldn't either).

Next to Democratic Senate staffers, industry respondents were the most negative towards economic incentive proposals. In fact, while charges may provide a cheaper way for *society* to meet given environmental goals, the *private* cost to industry of attaining these goals through charges might well turn out to be greater than the cost using standards. This is because firms would have to pay the government a charge for each unit of pollution emitted above zero; the total cost to the firm then becomes the cost of reducing pollution levels *plus* the cost of the charge on residual units of pollution. With standards, nothing must be paid beyond the cost of reducing pollution to the level of the standard. A firm for whom pollution reduction to the level of the standard was *very* expensive might save money by not having to meet the standard and abating pollution only to the point where the marginal cost of abatement equaled the charge, while paying the charge on residual units. But for many firms the combined cost of abating to the level where the marginal cost of abatement equaled the charge and then paying the charge on residual units would be greater than simply abating to the level of the standard. (This cost of paying the charge for residual units of pollution is a private cost to polluting firms. But charge payments, to an economist, are not a social cost, because taxes do not use up real resources, but only transfer them to the government, which can then distribute them in various ways.) Hardly a single industry respondent, however, had a sophisticated enough knowledge of charges to see the point that industry's private costs in a charges regime might indeed be greater than with standards, even when the social cost was less.

Tables 3-11 and 3-12, which display arguments and criticisms of charges proposals, do indicate, however, that the question of how much charges would cost industry was very much on re-spondents' minds. There were a number of generalized negative comments about pollution charges as "just another tax," combined with fears that the charge would be used to raise revenue (and thus the charge would be raised periodically for that purpose).

Table 3-11 Arguments Industry Officials Made for Charges

Argument	Percentage of Respondents Who Made Argument
Charges make it in one's self-interest to reduce pollution	35%
Internalize costs, "polluters should pay"	20
Encourage technical innovation	20
No advantages	15
Incentive to go beyond a standard	11
Promarket or antigovernment comment without further justification; general "prochoice" comment	10
Those with very high costs or slow response times are given an option; put constant pressure on all	10
Know no arguments	10
Stated efficiency argument but did not understand it well	5
Less bureaucracy, simplicity	5
Uniformity	5
"Based on cost-benefit considerations"	5
	(N = 20)

"Taxes could go higher and higher until they became confiscatory," one respondent argued. "I can see this being ratcheted down, becoming a never-ending moving target. The more you do, the more they ask you to do." Another pointed out that nearby Montgomery County in suburban Maryland had started using a tax on disposable bottles as a revenue generator. Some of the industry respondents did have an inkling of the fact that the private costs to them of charges might be greater than those of standards. "Currently, you don't have to abate your pollution below the standard, but an effluent tax is levied for every pound of pollution," one respondent said. "An effluent tax is in line with the zero discharge concept. It's a zero discharge regulation." Another pointed out that "the tax will continue even after correction of the pollution." A number of respondents expressed vague fears of a "double burden"—of having to lower pollution levels and then having to pay a tax on residual pollution as well.

Table 3-12   What Industry Saw as Disadvantages of Charges

Argument	Percentage of Respondents Who Made Argument
One should not have a choice of polluting if willing to pay a charge; "license to pollute"	25%
Dislike of money being spent as general revenues	25
Charges difficult to set; technical and economic information needed	20
Inequitable (would not allow variances); would hit the poor companies too hard; would concentrate industry	20
The government will set charges too high in order to raise revenue	15
Industry could just pass on costs and not control pollution	10
Industry uncertainty	10
Health damage should never be allowed; one cannot set a monetary value on health or the environment	5
Results are uncertain	5
	(N = 20)

The small minority of industry respondents who favored charges did so for ideological reasons. Gary Knight, the chief lobbyist on environmental issues for the U.S. Chamber of Commerce, came, unlike most of the industry environmental lobbyists, out of a political background as a staff member for a Republican congressman and as a HUD legislative liaison man during the Nixon administration. ("I loved the job because it gave me a chance to kick bureaucrats in the ass.") Knight said that he liked charges because "they're based on the economic method which most American businessmen understand, not on the hypocrisy that there's no threshold level below which there are no health effects or on the idea that we can get 95% abatement from everybody." He added that the Chamber of Commerce was opposed to charges, but that he would work to get the position changed if charges became a live issue. "But that will never happen. The EPA bureaucrats would stop it, because it would threaten their power."

Endnotes

1. I suspect that, were the interviews conducted today, the percentage would be up somewhat, but not dramatically.
2. *Congressional Record* (Senate), November 2, 1971, pp. 38826-34.
3. *Status of the Programs and Policies of the Environmental Protection Agency*, Hearing Before the Subcommittee on Environmental Pollution of the Committee on Public Works, United States Senate (Ninety-Fifth Congress, First Session), January 18, 1978, pp. 39–40.
4. *Air Pollution Control and Solid Waste Recycling*, Hearings Before the Subcommittee on Public Health and Welfare, Interstate and Foreign Commerce Committee, March 20, 1970, p. 642.

Chapter 4

POLITICAL STRATEGY
AND CHARGES

In this chapter, we switch gears again. Earlier, I discussed reasons for being concerned about proposals to introduce charges in environmental policy and presented the reactions of participants in environmental policymaking to charges proposals. In this chapter, I will take the perspective of an advocate of charges who, chastened by the arguments and findings of the earlier chapters, seeks to advance his cause in the political system.[1] I will be taking into consideration the arguments and findings of the rest of the book in developing a strategy for the charges advocate.

This chapter is also related to what preceded in another sense. Often, one of the problems with policy analysis done by economists is that it has a "missing chapter," a chapter that would outline a political strategy by which the proposals made in the analysis can be adopted and implemented. Part of the reason that economists have a difficult time being sensitive to issues of political strategy is that their training makes them ill-prepared to see the political importance of the battle for preferences. That training also makes them ill-prepared to understand the concerns of others who do not organize reality the way the microeconomic paradigm does. The broadening process that I seek to encourage in this book among those who are sympathetic to the microeconomic paradigm for analyzing public policy questions includes communicating a sense for issues of political strategy that are important for participants in public policy formation.

The Context of the Proposed Strategy

The interviews with participants in environmental policy making were held in 1978, and their comments on issues of political strategy as it relates to charges applied to the political environment of that time. The strategy to be presented in this chapter reflects the political situation at the time of the interviews; in effect, what I have done is to put myself in the shoes of an advocate of charges having the benefit of the empirical material gathered in 1978 and the normative material presented in the earlier chapters, and tried to develop a strategy suitable for that time.

The political environment at the time of the interviews remained more or less stable through the 1980 elections. That is, it was one where opposition to regulation was growing, but where environmentalists were rather well organized in Washington and had important political allies among the Democratic majority on the committees in the House and especially the Senate that were responsible for EPA. (The chairman of the Subcommittee on the Environment of the Senate Environment and Public Works Committee was, until early 1980, Edmund Muskie, "Mr. Clean Air.") This political environment changed dramatically after the election of 1980, which placed the Democrats in a minority in the Senate and put into key executive branch positions individuals with a far more critical attitude towards environmental regulation than their predecessors, Democratic or Republican, since the beginning of the wave of new environmental policies in the early 1970s.

The changed political environment means that the strategy to be outlined here would no longer, certainly in its details, be an appropriate one. It is therefore presented, not to suggest to charges advocates what they should be going out and doing right now, but to illustrate general points about political advocacy by applying them to a concrete situation. This is the technique used in teaching political advocacy in professional public policy programs, where students are asked to put themselves into a given, historical situation and to think through how they would have acted as advocates in that situation. It should be noted, however, that the political sea change that the 1980 elections brought about also serves as a reminder and a caution about the limitations of the type of strategizing that is taught in graduate public policy courses and commonly practiced in Washington. The limitation is that such strategizing tends to assume that a "business as usual" situation exists in which various participants in the process have more or less fixed power. This underestimates the changes that elections can bring about, for the assumptions don't work if a large, election-driven change occurs in the political system. Nevertheless, strategizing done in terms of Washington-based policy participants with relatively fixed power normally is valuable, because, usually, business *is* "as usual."

Another important change that took place after the interviews were completed was the moves by EPA, starting in 1979, to introduce aspects of the incentives approach into some environmental regulation, particularly through the "bubble" and "offsets" policies. The "bubble" policy applies to factories that have more than one source of a certain type of emission (say, particulates). It allows a firm to take the sum total of emissions that would have been allowed, under relevant EPA regulations, for the different sources of the pollutant in the factory, and comply with these overall levels using any combination of emissions reductions within the factory that the firm chooses. Thus, say a firm operates two processes in its factory for which the emission standards are ten and twenty units of emission, respectively. According to the bubble policy, as long as the factory's total emissions of the pollutant in question did not exceed thirty units, it wouldn't matter whether the firm achieved that goal through reductions to ten units at the first process and twenty at the second or to one unit at the first process and twenty-nine at the second. (This is called a "bubble" policy because the entire factory is treated as if there were a bubble placed over it; EPA doesn't care where the pollution reduction came from inside the bubble, as long as emissions don't exceed, in this hypothetical illustration, thirty units.) The "offsets" policy allows firms that plan increments in their emissions output, such as through building a new factory, to offset resultant pollution increases beyond a standard through equivalent emissions reductions from other sources the company owns.[2]

As implemented by EPA through the end of 1980, neither the offset nor the bubble policy represented the kind of radical change from standards to charges that economists traditionally have advocated. Both policies were centered within individual firms and covered certain limited types of emissions situations. This confined the efficiency advantages the policies were capable of obtaining.

Nevertheless, after so much beating against the wall for so many years, the adoption of the bubble and offset policies did represent a significant victory for advocates of efficiency in environmental regulation. Therefore, the final part of this chapter will briefly discuss how that change occurred, comparing the actual events with the strategy suggested earlier.

In the past, academic advocates of economic incentives seem to have thought only peripherally about specific strategies for getting their proposals adopted. They wrote articles and books on why charges would be a good idea. Beyond that, to the extent they had a strategy, it appeared to have had two elements. First, it involved talking to anyone who would listen about why charges were a good idea. Second, it involved recognition of the fact that a standards system was already in place and that it is more difficult to change something already in place than to forge something new, a recognition that led charges advocates to argue for use of economic incentive approaches in new areas of regulation.

With regard to the first element of the strategy, Allen Kneese, who was teaching at the University of New Mexico, stayed in frequent contact with staff people working for Senator Domenici of New Mexico, who sat on the environmental subcommittee of the Environment and Public Works Committee. Kneese got Domenici to express some interest in charges. Similarly, the initial contact between Senator Hart's staff and proeconomic incentive economists came via the wife of a Hart staffer, who was an economist working in the area. Such successes at access might appear serendipitous, but that may well be misleading: a classic strategy of the outsider is to use one asset he possesses in abundance—time—to knock on as many doors as possible, hoping to find somebody who answers. Successes attained this way may seem like a "lucky break"; actually, they often represent an extremely low success rate, given the large number of attempted contacts.

An advocate needs to do several things as he prepares a strategy for getting a decision he wishes to be adopted. He needs to understand who the participants in the policy-making process are and what their stands are likely to be. He needs to understand the procedure by which the decision is made and how the process distributes relative power advantages or disadvantages to various participants. (Changing the procedure may, therefore, be a tool an advocate has for changing the substantive outcome.) He needs an appreciation of the processes by which participants in a policy-making process influence each other.

To understand the stands of various participants in a policy-making process, one would wish to see what their personal values are and also, if appropriate, what kinds of stands their positions within large organizations encourage them to take. One would want to look at the mission of each organization and its standard operating procedures. (Thus one would expect EPA to oppose steps that would weaken its environmental mission or that would require changing ingrained standard operating procedures.) By providing information on the stands of various participants in environmental policymaking, the interview material presented in Chapter 3 would give insights into developing a strategy.

Thinking about the process of influencing other policy participants involves a number of things. First, it requires an appreciation for timing. The time at which a political issue is considered can affect the substantive outcome. It can do so by changing the "face" (to use Graham Allison's expression) an issue takes, that is, the aspect of a multifaceted issue that is perceived as most salient.[3] (Considering mine safety legislation right after a mining disaster will encourage the issue to be looked at in terms of safety protection; considering the same legislation during a period of inflation will encourage the issue to be looked at in terms of costs imposed.) Timing can also influence substantive outcomes because the balance of strength between supporters and opponents is different at different times. Second, thinking about the process of influencing others involves sensitivity to the order with which one proceeds in working to influence others. Some advocates, particularly outsiders, adopt a scattergun approach, but this is seldom successful, because it is difficult to influence all participants at once. But often, if some participants are brought around, they in turn will influence others who could not be brought around directly. The choice of whom to try to influence first, and of when to act, are both important. And so is attention to other methods of influence—from imposing a deadline for decision to skillfully using "outside" pressure on an organization.

Perhaps one of the most important methods the advocate uses to influence policy decisions is to try to get the issue to be seen in a way—to take a face—that will be most favorable to a decision he wants. And it is also this element of an advocate's approach that most distinguishes him from the image the policy analyst has of himself. It is common in politics, in issues where there are tradeoffs among conflicting values, for political advocates to talk mostly about the importance of the value they are arguing for, without confronting the tradeoff between it and conflicting values head on. Much political advocacy consists of such a pressing of the case for the value of one goal, while opponents press the case for the value of the conflicting goal. Thus, one set of political actors mourns the devastation wrought by unemployment, while another set paints a picture of the demoralizing results of inflation.

This feature of advocacy occurs for several reasons. Limitations of time and interest mean that most people won't be able to consider most issues seriously. Therefore, the aspect of the issue they happen to hear about will often influence importantly the choice they make, simply because other aspects are not on their minds at the time. Furthermore, decisions involving clearly articulated conflicting goals are often psychologically painful ones. It is painful to trade off, say, safety for cost. If one thinks only about one aspect of the choice—whether that aspect be safety or dollars—the choice is psychologically easier. For both these reasons, the face an issue takes (that is, what aspect of it is most salient) is important. The way people weigh conflicting values is not fixed. One's goal, then, if one wishes to promote a given choice, is often to get others to think about the positively regarded values realized by that choice and not to think about the negatively regarded ones the choice also happens to promote.

The analyst doubtless blanches at the approach of the policy advocate. He wishes that people would confront difficult tradeoffs head on. And he sees himself as presenting information about costs and benefits so that people can better make the necessary tradeoffs, not as influencing the outcome of decisions.

It is interesting to note that most analysts apply this strict and demanding attitude towards public but not private choices. It is not only public decisions that might be different if the strictures of the analyst—that we should confront difficult tradeoffs—were followed. Many decisions people make in their personal lives about things they buy might be far more difficult (and come out differently) if objectives that conflict with those the individual has in mind when making the purchase were articulated as clearly and forcefully as they often are in political debate. Decisions about buying chickens would be more difficult ones if pictures of the conditions under which chickens are commercially raised were repeatedly presented to people; decisions about travelling by air would be more difficult if consumers were to see pictures of plane wreckages as frequently as they see airline ads.

For an individual citizen, it might be a more urgent demand that he be asked to confront head-on the tradeoffs in, say, food purchases, because they represent a larger expenditure than the individual's share of the cost of environmental protection. Analysts are, however, generally less quick to demand that people be forced to be confronted with tradeoffs in their decisions as consumers than their decisions as citizens. Instead, they generally accept choices people make as consumers as "revealed preferences," and they often express disdain for those who criticize individual consumer choice as suboptimal. This gap between harsh criticism of insufficient analytical completeness in decision making about public matters and strong defense of the most extreme analytical incompleteness in decision making about private matters, even when the cost per citizen may be greater in the latter case than in the former case, strikes one as odd.

There are some justifications for such a gap, of course. One might argue that the degree of suboptimality of government decisions is greater than for private decisions, although I have not seen an empirical effort to justify that contention. Alternately, one may note that if one looks at the total impact on society of the decisions made by, say, the Administrator of EPA (that is, total rather than divided up on a per-citizen basis), these are indeed great. The costs of providing a decision maker with analysis that might allow him to make a better decision may be small compared to the benefits it brings. By contrast, the costs of getting out to a multitude of private decision makers the information that would allow them to make better decisions may well be much greater. My suspicion, nevertheless, is that part of the disparity in concern about suboptimal public and private decision making arises from a hostility with which many economists view governmental activities. (The suspicion could be tested by a hypothetical example. Imagine that decisions about environmental regulation were made by popular referendum. This would raise the costs of getting people the appropriate information for analytic thinking to the same level required to get them to think analytically in making

private decisions. Would most economists then abandon the effort
to bring about analytic thinking in the public decision making?)
Demands for detailed analysis by government, assuming such analysis is not currently being undertaken, allow those making the
demands to criticize or even ridicule government for its "irrationality." Furthermore, such demands increase the resources and
time required to make decisions, as well as placing an increased
burden on an activist government to look carefully before it leaps.
(To be sure, detailed analysis might *increase* the propensity of a
nonactivist government to act.) Efforts by economists to point out
the costs of environmental regulation have undoubtedly changed
"revealed preferences" (i.e., decisions) by bringing the cost aspect
of the choice more to the fore. It is the right, of course, of
economists to bring such cost information to the fore, as it is their
right to be skeptical of increased activities by government. But
it should be realized, again, that in acting this way economists
are participating in the battle for preferences, not simply taking
preferences as given.

Furthermore, and even more importantly, the analyst's self-
image as someone who encourages people to confront conflicting
values but does not seek to influence the content of those values
is not a correct portrayal of his own role. Economists advocating
use of charges in environmental policy make an argument based
on the efficiency advantages of charges. Sometimes "efficiency"
is presented as a neutral objective that everyone can be "for."
And, indeed everybody *is* "for" efficiency in the sense that they
would prefer achieving a given goal for less money than for more
money. But whenever there are tradeoffs between efficiency and
other goals, the consensus favoring efficiency disappears. This is
obvious in the huge number of political issues involving tradeoffs
between efficiency and equity. But it also applies to moving from
a standards-based to a charges-based approach to environmental
regulation. If one believes that taxing rather than regulating pollution has various disadvantages, along some dimension other than
efficiency, then one must ask oneself how much (if any) of one's
other goals one is willing to give up in order to get more efficiency.
And even if one has no substantive objections to charges, one
must still, if charges are not already in place, give up *time* that
could otherwise be spent working for the attainment of other
environmental policy. What economists must be—indeed, what

they are when they work for charges—is *lobbyists for efficiency,* trying to influence people's preferences just the way other advocates do. They compete against other advocates to get people to attribute a high weight to one favored value among several conflicting goals. They are trying to *make efficiency the face of the issue* that people think about when they make a decision.

A Strategy for Charges Advocates: Focusing on Environmentalists and EPA

At the time the interviews with participants in environmental policy making were conducted, economists who advocate charges were not influential within EPA, Congress, or the environmental or industry lobbying organizations. But they did have access to journals, magazines, and to well-regarded policy "think tanks" such as the Brookings Institute and the American Enterprise Institute. They also had gained a foothold in the environmental decision-making process through the efforts of the Carter administration to gain greater influence over regulatory decisions. Upon entering the White House, the Carter administration made "regulatory reform" a priority and put economists in the Council of Economic Advisors, the Council on Wage and Price Stability, and later the newly created Regulatory Analysis Review Group in charge of those regulatory reform efforts. (Charles Schultze became head of the Council of Economic Advisors.)

Charge advocates, therefore, had two ways to influence the policy-making process—through the persuasive impact of their ideas and through their role in White House regulatory efforts. I noted earlier that a sense of *timing*—that is, a feeling for which participants in a policy formation process to "go after" when—is an important part of good advocacy. I believe that the situation for charges advocates in 1978 would have suggested strongly that the places to start were among environmentalist lobbyists and with EPA itself.

We may note briefly the reasons for this conclusion. Among the nonbureaucratic participants in environmental policy making, Republican staffers, it is true, were more favorable to charges than environmentalists. But it would have been questionable whether that could have been translated into support by Republican members of Congress for the statutory changes that a major move from standards to charges would require. Republican *politicians,* as opposed to the more ideological committee staff members, are likely to be less enamored of economic incentive proposals simply because they like the market. The senior Republican staff member of the Senate Subcommittee on the Environment noted in the interview with him that "Republicans are more amenable to market mechanisms, and some Republicans might be for this as a way to let industry off the hook." But he continued by noting that "they would be opposed if it would make things more difficult for industry." (They would also, he added, look carefully at the effect of such proposals on their particular states.) Furthermore, the Republicans were in the minority in Congress and out of power in the White House. They did not dominate the political agenda, and they needed to husband their efforts for attacks that would gain quick political resonance. This made them unlikely candidates for the role of educators about a new concept several steps removed from the center of national concerns.

Environmentalists were not as sympathetic to charges as were the Republican staffers, but they were the next most sympathetic group. It may be noted that environmentalists and industry respondents were both asked in our survey which groups would be most likely to support charges proposals if they were introduced before Congress and which groups would oppose them. The dominant view among *both* industry and environmentalists was that industry would oppose such proposals and environmentalists would favor them, although the tendency to see environmentalists as supportive was less among environmentalists than among industry respondents. Environmentalists were also the most knowledgeable about charges. Finally, environmentalists, if persuaded to support charges, would have been in a position to influence both Democratic staffers—and hence the Democratic Congressional majority—and the EPA.

As for EPA, one would not, if one attempted to predict the stand of the organization from its organizational interests, have expected it to be a source for initiatives for incentive approaches. One would have expected the enforcement bureaucracy in the agency to resist sharing its responsibility with the Internal Revenue Service (in charge of collecting all taxes), an agency without any environmental mission. One would have predicted that many agency officials would share the concerns that Democratic staffers and environmentalists had about charges. One would also have predicted that, since EPA would have had to bear the brunt of the organizational learning that a switchover to a new system would imply, the agency would have had special reasons for hostility.

As a good first approximation, especially if one has little additional information, a prediction of organizational stands based on organizational interests is generally a good one. Further information about the specific people occupying various positions can often, however, provide a more nuanced picture of the situation within an organization. As it happened, there were at the time at EPA individuals at the top of the agency—such as Administrator Douglas Costle and one of his most important deputies, William Drayton—who were sympathetic to new approaches that could be packaged under the politically appealing rubric of "regulatory reform." (Drayton had had significant exposure to the ideas of academic economists on environmental policy and had in fact written on the subject of economic incentives.) Furthermore, the growing regulatory analysis staff at EPA consisted, in significant measure, of economists who could be expected to be in-house advocates.

To be sure, those at the top who might have been sympathetic to economic incentive approaches could not have counted on success in changing policy, especially if the costs of such changes in terms of lowered morale or other problems with the career staff were too great. The strategy in such a situation might have been to use "pressure" from the White House economists outside the agency to facilitate the process of change within the agency. An important general lesson for the advocate to learn is that frequently the way in which "outside pressure" works to change an organization is via the invigorating effect the pressure has on people already within the organization who advocate the changes the outsiders seek. Faced with pressure from the White House, proponents of change could be in a position to say to skeptics within the agency, in effect, "we'd better make these changes, or else, given all the pressure, something even worse will happen." The outside pressure would thus have weakened the position of those inside who might otherwise have resisted.

Making the Case to Environmentalists

The strategy for making environmentalists into supporters of charges would, I think, have been a twofold one. One tack would have been to impress them strongly with the efficiency advantages of charges over standards. What one would then have been asking them to do would be to be willing to trade off the costs they perceived of going to charges against the efficiency advantages. The second tack would have been a more or less straightforward political "deal." Economists advocating charges might have agreed to call off their criticisms of what many of them felt to be the excessive levels of protection environmental regulations were de-manding—criticisms that shot straight against the central concerns of environmentalists—in exchange for environmentalist support for charges—support that involved the question at the center of the environmental policy agenda of most economists. Such a "deal" would have involved the archetypical principle of logrolling, that people agree to support each other's issue of primary concern, while abandoning their opposition on an issue of secondary concern.

I will devote most of my attention here to the first possible tack for dealing with environmentalists. The logrolling approach would, I suspect, have been repugnant to most economists, who regard themselves as dealing in the world of ideas and are therefore averse, as part of a "deal," to remaining silent on ideas they believe in.[4] Furthermore, since economists are not an organized or disciplined group, it is unlikely that such a "deal" would have been able to stick; other economists, not part of the deal, would doubtless have continued to criticize environmental regulations whose costs they believed outweighed their benefits.

As for the first approach towards environmentalists—persuading the environmentalists to have been willing to accept other costs in order to attain the efficiency benefits of charges—the outcome of any judgment trading off efficiency benefits against philosophical or strategic costs could not have been assumed in advance. The use of charges raises, as has been noted, profound issues of what kind of society we wish to live in. Furthermore, it should be remembered that the advantage, say, of living in a society where it is considered criminal to pollute is one that is a public good — it can be shared by everyone without becoming dissipated. The costs per individual of efficiency losses, by contrast, become much smaller because they are divided among the whole population. Thus each $1 billion efficiency loss costs only about $5 per citizen, a modest sum for morality, if that is one's morality. (The moral benefits might be concentrated to a certain segment of the population, such as active environmentalists, and the costs widely dispersed. In this case there exists a classic instance of the familiar proposition about the difficulty efficiency-based policies have gaining adoption because their benefits are dispersed while their costs —moral costs in this case—are concentrated.)

There were, furthermore, important *strategic* costs that many environmentalists perceived in moving from standards to charges. A strategic cost is a cost in terms of the success a group has in achieving its main goal—in this case, achievement by environmentalists of requirements for high levels of environmental cleanup.

Having a strategy is a key part of successful advocacy. Advocates in the political process, such as the environmental lobbyists and Democratic staffers we interviewed, must, if they are to be successful in their work, develop an appreciation for strategic considerations. And, indeed, the interview responses by these groups indicated that a significant part of their fear of charges was strategic in nature. Twenty-six percent of environmentalists stated that one disadvantage of charges was that it would be politically difficult to set them high enough; another five percent listed as a disadvantage the argument that reopening environmental legislation (something that would have been required in order to grant government authority to set pollution charges) would have produced less stringent environmental laws, because the political climate was less favorable to the environment than when the laws were passed.

It should surprise nobody, although it is sometimes forgotten when discussing the difficulties of arousing interest in economic incentive proposals, that the overriding concern of environmentalist and industry lobbyists is to work for adoption of environmental laws and regulations reflecting what they consider to be appropriate requirements for levels of cleanup. Environmentalists spend most of their time fighting for stricter cleanup demands, which produce more improvement in environmental quality; industry spends most of its time fighting for more lenient cleanup demands, which produce smaller cost burdens. In answer to an early survey question on criticisms of environmental policy, by far the most common criticism cited by both environmentalists and industry respondents was that environmental regulation called for inappropriate levels of protection, with industry believing that the level was too high and environmentalists believing that it was too low. This criticism was cited by 84% of environmentalist respondents (N = 19) and 85% of the industry respondents (N = 20). The next most common criticisms were mentioned by no more than one-quarter of the respondents.

Moving from standards to charges would change in several respects the way environmental issues are considered in the political system. Environmentalists cited several reasons why such changes might produce a lowering of the level of cleanup demands. First, reopening environmental statutes to amendment would likely produce statutory language less favorable to environmentalists than existing language. Second, debate on the stringency of environmental demands that is phrased in terms of "what should the level of a charge be?" focuses attention on costs and thus hurts environmentalists, while a debate that is phrased in terms of "what should a standard be?" focuses attention on health protection and thus helps environmentalists. Furthermore, the very move from standards to charges, as noted earlier, removes a stigmatization of polluting behavior that is one way to influence citizens to believe that high levels of cleanup should be demanded.

The first concern reflected a sensitivity to the importance of timing in influencing political outcomes. The current air and water environmental statutes were adopted (in 1970 and 1972) at a time when public support for the environmental movement was at its height and before a counteroffensive, aided by energy and inflation problems, could be organized. The statutes adopted required standards to be set, and they did not authorize the establishment of charges. A move towards charges in the air and water areas would, therefore, require statutory changes. Environmentalists had survived surprisingly well the political battles between 1975 and 1977 that produced amendments to the Clean Air Act and the Water Pollution Control Act, which were finally passed in 1977. But the battles were scarring ones, and environmentalists suffered some defeats. The fear was that a major reopening of environmental legislation to remove the requirement that standards be set and to establish authorization to set charges would have risked reopening the statutes for other sorts of amendment as well and, environmentalists feared, a weakening of those basic statutes. (The grounds for this fear may have declined with the increasing tendency to use the congressional reauthorization process, which occur automatically and with regularity, to open statutes for revision. Indeed, the scheduled 1981 reauthorization of the Clean Air Act, debate on which is about to begin as these lines are being written, will certainly open the statute to the possibility of revision. In a reinterview in 1981, one of those environmentalists most worried about the "reopening" issue stated that he still felt that environmentalists would want to minimize the amount of reopening; he was also afraid that it would be easier to hide a weakening of the statute under the guise of a move to charges.)

A second strategic concern was that moving to charges might produce an environmental debate that centered on costs. Such a concern demonstrates the importance to advocates of the "face" an issue takes. Both "saving health" and "saving money" are values that are widely regarded positively. Environmentalists and industry representatives both know this. Seeking, as they do, laws and regulations that reflect different levels of environmental protection, both environmentalists and industry advocates realize that they want to get people to think about the aspect of environmental regulation that best promotes the choice they would hope to see people make. What some environmentalists in our interviews were worried about was that if environmental policy were set using charges, debates would be over the monetary amount of charge levels. This would in turn inevitably make people think more about costs than otherwise. Debates on standards can be phrased— and by environmentalists are phrased—in a way that presents a favorable face: for example, "What is required to protect public health?"

A third aspect of the strategic argument against charges that some environmentalists expressed was the view that using taxes would transfer committee jurisdiction over environmental legislation in Congress from the committees where it presently lay to the congressional tax-writing committees—Finance in the Senate, and Ways and Means in the House. Accounts by advocates of economic incentives of the political difficulties of charges proposals not infrequently make reference to these jurisdictional consequences. But the implication is left that the source of opposition to such a shift comes simply from the self-interest of members of the committees who have power over such legislation and hence could be expected to oppose proposals that would limit their authority. Such an account fosters the throw-up-one's-hands approach to the political system that many academic economists tend to take anyway—a view that the rationality of economists' proposals flounders on the irrationality of politics. If one places the enormity of the efficiency advantages of charges against the paltriness of the desires of members of certain committees to retain personal power, the political system does indeed come out looking worthy of any contempt heaped upon it.

But things would not have been that simple. In fact, the concern about changed committee jurisdiction demonstrates the effect that different procedures have on substantive outcomes by distributing power advantages and disadvantages to different participants. Committees have significant influence over the specific content of legislation eventually passed by the entire Congress. They can prevent bills from ever being considered on the floor. Members of Congress not on a committee frequently defer to the judgment of the committee on a bill. These features in turn become rational given our political system. In our system, unlike the situation in countries with parliamentary government and strong party discipline, the legislature gives bills genuine consideration, rather than automatically passing every bill the executive sends up. This genuine consideration requires that there exist some gatekeeping function so that congressmen will not be swamped with bills to vote on, and also some specialization of tasks so that the members have time to develop the expertise to evaluate properly a piece of legislation. Such specialization would be useless unless there were some deference to the results of that expert consideration. For both these reasons, in the context of a legislature that wishes to give bills genuine consideration, the unusual influence that committees have makes good sense.

Furthermore, it is not surprising that in different committees there should often be different dominant views on certain issues. Committees often tend to attract strong advocates (and, sometimes, strong opponents as well) of policy in a substantive area. Thus the agriculture committees tend to attract farm representatives who favor programs to aid farmers, and the labor committees tend to attract urban representatives (on the Democratic side at least) who favor programs to aid workers. If different committees have different dominant viewpoints on an issue, and the committee out of which a bill comes has an important influence over the final content of the bill, then the jurisdiction of one committee or another over a bill may well change significantly a bill's final content.

This was what environmentalists were concerned about when they worried about the implications of moving from standards to charges for committee jurisdiction. The environmental committees were filled with environmentalists—most prominently, at the time of the research, Senator Muskie and Congressman Paul Rogers. The chairmen of the tax-writing committees were Russell Long and Al Ullman. Neither of the latter two was particularly favorable to environmental issues. Fear that environmental legislation emerging from such committees would have mandated lower degrees of environmental protection—not mere concerns over loss of personal power by members of existing committees—dominated the concerns of environmentalists and their congressional allies about jurisdiction.

The very first thing Karl Braithwaite, the Democratic staff director for the Senate committee, said in the course of a long interview was, "The first thing I ask economists is, 'Do you think environmental policy would be in better hands if it was under Russell Long?' " Probably part of the reason that he mentioned this so soon was to suggest that economists are impractical and do not consider "real world" implications of their theories. In any case, a concern about committee jurisdiction was clearly on Braithwaite's mind. Tariffs, he continued, were not intended as a revenue-raising measure, yet they went to the tax-writing committees. Braithwaite also went on to add that "Muskie hasn't approached the issue that way," and that it "isn't Leon's first concern." Indeed, Leon Billings said in an interview that "the salient issue isn't jurisdiction. It's that effluent charges are a lousy idea. My experience on jurisdiction has always been that if you believe in something and are intelligent, you can do an end run."

Industry and environmentalist respondents were asked their reaction to a possible change in committee jurisdiction resulting from a move from standards to charges. *Both* groups agreed that such a change would favor industry and hurt environmentalists. Of environmentalist respondents, 23% (N = 13) stated they wouldn't care one way or another if there were a shift in juris-diction. Among those who *did* care, 100% reacted negatively to the idea of such a change. Of the industry respondents, a much larger 47% (N = 15) didn't care, but of those who did care, 63% (N = 8) had a positive reaction and 37% a negative reaction (because the existing committees, they said, had developed ex-pertise). Many of the industry people doubted whether any trans-fer of jurisdiction would take place. ("Muskie has enough seniority so that if you move the environment to Finance, Muskie will go to Finance.") But there was little opposition to the prospect, if it could be arranged. "We could probably get further in arguments on the merits with Russell Long than with Muskie and Rogers," one of the most important industry lobbyists told me. "When you walk into Public Works, all they care about is health." Responded another: "The business community would love it. It would be great to have Russell Long."

Interestingly, however, there was no tendency for those en-vironmentalists worried about committee jurisdiction to be less sympathetic to charges than those who didn't care. A crosstabu-lation of attitudes on charges with attitudes on committee ju-risdiction showed no differences between the two groups of environmentalists. Similarly, although changing a procedure for considering an issue is one tool an advocate may use to get sub-stantive decisions more favorable to his position, such consider-ations did not produce any industry support for charges based on hopes of getting more favorable committee consideration. Sup-porting charges for that reason was inhibited by skepticism that such a jurisdictional transfer would take place, combined with a general failure to consider strategic implications of charges for industry, given a lack of thought about the issue. A number of industry respondents volunteered that they had never considered the impact of a move from standards to charges on committee jurisdiction before the question was asked them in our survey.[5]

There was a final reason why environmentalists might be wor-ried that a move to charges might produce a lower level of de-mands for environmental cleanup. In a situation where actors in the environmental policy process would have to spend *time* work-ing for a shift from current regulatory approaches towards new ones, there may be elements of a "prisoner's dilemma" game. Imagine that industry and environmentalists might each value efficiency enough to devote 20% of their time working for greater efficiency in regulation, a goal on which both sides agree, while 80% of their time went to their other goals, on which there is disagreement. Each side may be afraid, however, that any time spent on working for a goal on which both sides agree may, unless the other side is willing to spend equal time working for the goal, become net time subtracted from working for the goals on which there is disagreement, thus increasing the chances that one's opponent will prevail in those areas. Both sides may then fail to spend any time working for efficiency. A less efficient result than anybody desires may thus be produced.

Many of these themes regarding strategic worries about a switchover to charges appeared in the interviews with two of the most influential environmentalist respondents—a senior official of one of the most respected environmentalist groups and Karl Braithwaite, then majority staff chief for the Senate Subcommittee on Environmental Pollution. Both expressed significant concern in the interviews with the impact of a switch to charges on the level of protection environmental regulation demanded.

The senior environmentalist expressed his concerns in a poignant and forceful way. It was clear that he had read the charges literature carefully; he had a sophisticated understanding of the efficiency and other arguments for charges. Yet he was worried about the consequences of opening up the environmental laws to amendment at a time when the environmental movement was less strong than it had been:

> *I have never been willing to go to the Hill and advocate a charges approach. This is because of the larger politics of the issue. We got the Clean Air Act enacted at the high point of the environmental issue. We've been trying to defend the Clean Air Act, and therefore we're not willing to go to the Hill and say, "let's change the whole system." If the whole system is up for grabs, you'd get a lot less in the law than we have now.* Getting charges under those circumstances would mean you'd get a more efficient system to achieve a hell of a lot less [*emphasis added*].

The same respondent also presented a version of the "prisoner's dilemma" problem alluded to earlier:

> *I said to an industrial audience recently that this system is too complicated, but as long as every time Congress decides to legislate on the issue you oppose any regulation, I can't go up and advocate a system which is less complicated. . . . As long as there is confrontation, you can't have charges.*

He continued saying that he would work for charges if environmentalists and industry could agree that reopening the environmental legislation to get charges established would not be used
as an occasion to reopen the legislation to get levels of protection
revised.

The same respondent was also concerned with the political
impact of the economic language of charges:

> *Charges give you a weaker weapon to fight with. The political battle
> gets fought out with symbols that are stronger for industry and
> weaker for us. You can't talk money, because that's their game. The
> political process is such that we have to talk health, and they talk
> money. We can't have a debate on money, because we lose. If
> there's a debate on public health, we win.*

For these strategic reasons as well as the ideological ones discussed earlier, then, the outcome of a balancing judgment whereby
environmentalists might have been persuaded to accept the costs
of the various disadvantages of charges in exchange for their efficiency benefits should not have been assumed in advance. Nevertheless, I believe that many environmentalists might have been
willing to make the tradeoff, at least for new areas of regulation
and for changes that would not require statutory modifications,
where some of the strategic considerations would become less
salient. What would have been required for charge supporters
would have been a strategy that gave key attention to *assuring
that environmentalists became aware of the efficiency argument
for charges,* an awareness that our interviews showed was, as of
1978, present only to a limited degree.

Environmentalists who had opposed charges and who had failed
to mention efficiency as an argument for charges were asked:

> *Assuming it could be demonstrated to you that we could, in fact,
> obtain any given degree of environmental quality for 20% less cost
> to society using charges than by using standards, would this fact
> be sufficient to overcome your objections to a charges approach?*

Five of eight said they would then favor charges. Four of those
five would still have been willing to favor charges even if there
were a 10% risk that such savings would not materialize and that,
instead, charges "turn out to work worse than our current system
of environmental regulation." (By contrast, only three of seven
congressional committee majority staffers were willing to support

charges if they proved to cost 20% less, and only one of those three would still have favored the change under the risky alternative.)[6] Likewise, when environmentalist opponents of charges were asked, "What, if any, new information would make you change your point of view on charges?" three of the four environmentalists responded that an example of the successful use of charges would convince them. (By contrast, three of the six industry opponents who were asked the same question replied that a demonstration that charges were cheaper for industry would be required to convince them, while another two said that a convincing argument by an economist would do so.)

A final point would have needed to be kept in mind when trying to make an argument for charges to environmentalists. Many economists who advocate charges also believe that environmental regulation has demanded too high a level of reduction of environmental pollution. This belief is not *logically* linked to support for charges, although there tends to be a spurious correlation due to common causation via the microeconomic paradigm. Considering that economists advocate both charges and (frequently) lower levels of environmental protection, it should not have been surprising that many environmentalists confused the two criticisms. The frequently expressed objection environmentalists registered against charges—that it was impossible to place a monetary price on health or the environment—was an objection to the economist view that environmental regulation showed insufficient sensitivity to costs as well as to charges as a tool of environmental policy. Furthermore, in another question environmentalists were asked whether use of the term "cost-effective" in describing a proposal made them more or less sympathetic to it. The term "cost-effective," as used by economists, applies to the measure that will achieve a given goal at the lowest cost. Thus, economists would say that charges are a more cost-effective means of pollution reduction than standards. But it developed from responses in the survey that most environmentalists confused the term "cost-effective" with the term "cost-benefit"—and they showed, in general, skepticism or hostility towards cost-benefit analysis, which they tended to dismiss as "an industry tool." Thus charges might well have been associated in the minds of many environmentalists with criticisms of the levels of protection environmental regulations required. (One respondent, in spontaneously bringing up *The Public Use of Private Interest*, said that Schultze "seemed to be reflecting the concerns of the business community.")

One of the ways ideologies work to aid people organize reality is to encourage them to look favorably at the ideas of "friends" and unfavorably at the ideas of "enemies." There is a widespread view among policy participants, for instance, that expert studies by "enemies" may be disregarded, on the theory that a study reaching an opposite conclusion by an expert "friend" can always be found. There is little attempt, in other words, to evaluate such studies on their merits.[7] To the extent that economists would have been seen as "enemies" of environmentalists because of their criticisms of "excessive" environmental demands, environmentalists would have doubtless been less inclined to evaluate what economists said on the merits.

If the best chance for getting environmentalists (and possibly congressional Democratic staffers) to change their minds would have been to make them understand the efficiency advantages of charges, then the explanation for why the efficiency argument had not penetrated more environmentalist heads becomes important. Part of the explanation is probably relatively straightforward. For someone who has never studied economics, efficiency arguments, even when presented in simple, nonmathematical form, may be unfamiliar and therefore complicated. Also, as noted earlier, one of the best-known arguments for economic incentive approaches in regulatory policy, *The Public Use of Private Interest* by Charles Schultze, underemphasized the efficiency argument.

Beyond these explanations, though, there is the more subtle and interesting one, involving the role of ideology as an organizing principle for stimuli a person receives, that was discussed in the Introduction to this book. The focus on the problems of misperception or failure to perceive that ideologies create has up to now mainly involved failures that microeconomic ideology encourages. This focus should be broadened. For just as their ideology discourages microeconomists from perceiving the philosophical problems with charges that many noneconomists have, so too does the ideology of many environmentalists, with its unease about markets, discourage them from perceiving the efficiency arguments economists make.

Except for the industry respondents, most of the other respondents in our survey appeared to have had well-developed general ideologies. And one could see how these ideologies helped organize the stimuli they received, in a way that, in the absence of ideological moorings, responses lost the organization they otherwise would have had. This could be seen in different responses from environmentalists regarding their attitudes towards standards versus charges approaches for limiting driving in downtown areas, on the one hand, and solid waste problems caused by packaging materials, on the other. Environmentalists and Senate majority staffers were asked whether, in transportation control plans to reduce driving in center cities, they would prefer parking bans and other direct restrictions, or parking surcharges and increased bridge tolls. Only two environmentalists favored surcharges, while six favored direct restrictions. (Three favored "both.") This was a higher proportion of opponents for economic incentive approaches than was the case for economic incentives for air and water pollution. Yet, in stark contrast, nine of ten environmentalists questioned (and all three Senate majority staffers) favored proposals for a product charge added to the price of packaging material rather than standards restricting excessive packaging. There are several possible explanations for this difference, but one in particular is relevant in this context. In the case of transportation control plans, there had been little propaganda by economists for why charges were a superior approach for traffic restriction. So the generalized skepticism about markets many environmentalists felt showed through, unalloyed by economist counterarguments. In the case of packaging, the product charge issue had become identified with environmentalists (and opposition identified with industry). This allowed environmentalists to organize their response along familiar ideological lines of "good guys" and "bad guys."

Given the organizing role of ideologies, it is not surprising that when respondents heard an expression such as "use the market," an ideological automatic pilot took over to guide them over the mountains and through the fog. But, in using the ideology, information that did not fit the organizing principles was also filtered out. *It would seem that, thanks to ideology, some of the survey respondents simply did not register efficiency arguments for charges in their brains because they did not fit into the organizing principles they used.*

As supporters of charges have on occasion lamented, those involved in the formulation of environmental policy have difficulty perceiving things through the organizing principles the microeconomic paradigm applies because few of them have backgrounds in economics. This observation was confirmed in our interviews. The largest group of respondents were lawyers. But their percentage was a relatively modest 34% (N = 61), and the number of scientists and engineers was only 1% less. The next largest group (23%) was political scientists and other social scientists, and then came those whose only job had been in politics, agency work, or on Capitol Hill. There was not a single economist among the respondents.

Earlier in this chapter, a second part of a strategy for charge opponents was suggested, namely a "deal" whereby economists would have traded abandoning criticism of excessive levels of environmental regulatory demands in exchange for environmentalist support for charges. Absent a willingness of charge advocates to "deal" in that fashion, it might have been possible for charges advocates to suggest to environmentalists, once they were made aware of the cost-saving features of charges, that they make what might have been seen as an "internal deal" with themselves: they would advocate charges to head off demands from environmental opponents for lowering the levels of environmental protection that government policy required. (Indeed, once aware of the efficiency advantages of charges, environmentalists might see such reasons for coming to advocate charges by themselves, without the necessity of suggestions from others.) Growing hostility to the costs of government regulation would have provided an opportunity to supporters of charges to point out to environmentalists that embracing charges would provide them a way to defend environmentalist goals against attack. The efficiency advantages of charges would allow attainment of the same level of environmental cleanup at less cost, thus reducing costs as critics demanded, while maintaining the protection levels environmentalists sought. Furthermore, a change in the system of regulation could have been presented as an example of "regulatory reform," a popular political slogan.

Developments Relating to Economic Incentives in Environmental Policy Through November 1980

As noted earlier in this chapter, moves toward initiation of some kinds of economic incentive policies were taken by EPA in 1979 and 1980. The moves originated almost entirely from within EPA. Neither environmentalists nor EPA's congressional allies played any significant role in urging such steps on EPA; those quarters ranged from mild skepticism to mild support.

Those within EPA who promoted the changes did in fact appear to follow much of the strategy outlined above. They used outside pressure from White House economists to help reduce resistance within the agency.[8] They touted the changes as examples of how the Carter Administration was responding to demands for "regulatory reform." And they appeared to be trying to use the changes partly to stave off demands for lowering the level of protection environmental regulation mandated.

Several aspects of the bubble and offset policies, which I did not catch in my proposed strategy for the charges advocate but that did, I think, ease the acceptance of the EPA initiatives, should be noted. The first is that, because of the way the bubble and offset policies were formulated, many of the problems with economic incentives on dimensions other than efficiency—such as the setting of a price on environmental quality or the encouragement of self-interest—were largely avoided. Neither new policy required setting a price on pollution. Neither policy needed to be launched with paeans to the public use of private interest. Both policies were instead presented, in a quite straightforward way, as ways to achieve attainment of an environmental standard at a lower cost. (To be sure, these gains are achieved at the expense of making the bubble and offset policies less advantageous on efficiency grounds than charges.) It is tempting to believe that the originators of the policies felt—at least intuitively—that they were making the tradeoff between efficiency advantages and moral disadvantages much less painful by doing so. Economists probably would not, in general, have appreciated the difference that change might make; agency managers with political experience would be more likely to do so. A second factor that probably eased acceptance of the change within EPA was that, since the bubble and offset policies did not require setting a charge, the IRS was not brought in as an enforcement agency. The new policies also gave EPA enforcement people ample work investigating bubble and offset proposals.

A Final Note

The victory of Ronald Reagan in the 1980 elections, as well as the changes in Congress, changed a number of the assumptions on which the discussion of political strategies in this chapter was based. This makes the strategic discussion, as noted earlier, mainly of historical interest—although history does, indeed, have interest. A brief word might be noted in conclusion about the implications of the election-impelled changes for charge advocates. (These words are being written as the debate over the reauthorization of the Clean Air Act is about to begin.)

The change in administration dramatically increased the power of industry over the regulatory process and decreased that of environmentalists. The power of economists over the process increased as well. The election results might make environmentalists more anxious to advocate charges as an alternative to scaling back the protectiveness of regulatory demands. They might, however, become so involved in a trench warfare effort to prevent major rollbacks in environmental legislation that they would find themselves unwilling to take the chance of diverting any of their energies into a battle for charges. Industry, in our analysis, was never likely to favor charges under any circumstances. This leaves the economists, newly empowered but still unlikely to bring about major changes themselves. One question is how much of their own energies they wish to devote—*vis-à-vis* both Congress and the EPA—to promoting charges as opposed to promoting "regulatory relief" for industry.

There is certain in 1981 to be an important debate over how strict clean air legislation should be. The question is whether—as in past times when the subject of the debate has centered on the stringency of environmental demands—the issue of economic incentive approaches may again get lost in the shuffle.

Endnotes

1. For a discussion of the politics of charges by a political scientist, see Russell B. Stevenson, "The Politics of Charges," in Frederick R. Anderson et al., *Environmental Improvement Through Economic Incentives* (Baltimore: Johns Hopkins University Press, 1977).
2. See Timothy B. Clark, "New Approaches to Federal Regulation," *National Journal*, 11 (August 11, 1979) and William Drayton, "Economic Law Enforcement," *Harvard Environmental Law Review*, 4 (January 1980).
3. This terminology appears in *The Essence of Decision* (Boston: Little, Brown, 1971), p. 168.
4. There is some irony in the likely repugnance economists would feel about such "deals," considering their strong conceptual resemblance to the voluntary exchange model.
5. Related to the suggestion that charges hadn't gotten further because of the personal power interests of members of the existing environmental committees was the suggestion, presented frequently at the time by charge advocates, that neither environmentalists nor industry lobbyists were willing to advocate charges for fear of offending the powerful subcommittee chairman (Senator Muskie) and his powerful staff chief (Leon Billings). This was also a "throw up your hands" view, in that it suggested that crass political considerations were interfering with good policy making. It should therefore be noted that the interviews did not support the notion that this was a wide concern. Of nine environmentalists asked about Muskie's views on charges, five responded they didn't know what they were and another two thought that Muskie favored charges (or that he had mixed feelings).
6. Note that this difference constitutes another argument that charge advocates should have addressed their attention first to environmentalists rather than to Democratic staffers.
7. For an interesting discussion, see David Seidman, "The Politics of Policy Analysis," *Regulation*, 1 (July 1977).
8. By contrast, at OSHA there was nobody within the agency who wished to promote economic incentive approaches to occupational safety and health, and "regulatory reform" at OSHA consisted mainly of repeal of some outmoded (and seldom-enforced) regulations.

Chapter 5

CONCLUSION

Traditionally, much political debate in society has revolved around two types of issues. One type is the "who gets what" issues that are generally framed in the public debate as questions of equity—although interests as well as ideas are clearly involved in such debate. Thus, societies debate issues about whether to undertake programs of help to the elderly, or the poor, or farmers, or small businessmen, or flood victims. A second type of issue is what kinds of values people hold. Thus, societies debate what is happening to the work ethic, whether people are excessively materialistic, whether family values are declining, or how blacks and whites feel about each other.

"Policy analysis" done using the microeconomic paradigm seeks to effect what can only be called a revolution in the topics for political debate. For such policy analysis tries to draw conclusions about what public policies are desirable: (1) without taking equity considerations in account in particular policy areas (leaving them to one-time cash transfers); and (2) taking preferences as givens and seeking an optimizing solution based on given preferences.

In fact, as I have pointed out in several contexts in earlier chapters, the second part of the exercise—to develop policy recommendations, taking preferences as given—is simply impossible even if it were desirable. By undertaking the kind of analysis they do, microeconomics-influenced policy analysts themselves seek to influence people's preferences in at least five important ways discussed in the course of this book. They seek to influence people's preferences: (1) away from caring about preferences (which is a preference itself); (2) away from caring about equity issues in the design in public policies; (3) towards ascribing greater weight to

153

efficiency goals in public policy decisions; (4) towards a sympathy
for self-interest as a motivation for human behavior; and (5) by
favoring market exchanges, towards increased calculativeness and
decreased value imputed to various nonpriced things. The microeconomic agenda is pregnant with implications for people's
preferences.

Much of the argument in this book has revolved in one way
or another around the contention that microeconomic analysis pays
insufficient attention either to things that go on inside people's
heads or to the influence that the debates and decisions of political
life have over people's values. The microeconomic agenda is one
in which public policy making is denuded of some of the most
important features of politics—politics in the best sense of the
battle over what kind of society we are going to create.

In a way, this sort of policy analysis may be seen as scholarship
for the "Me generation." A time of cynicism about not only public
officials but public life as well, such as has existed in the United
States during the past decade, is a fertile time for ideas that lack,
in my view, an adequate appreciation or understanding of the role
of public life. These doctrines not only reflect the cynicism, but
also reinforce it as well. Such doctrines fail to give weight to other
ideas that would nudge people in a different direction. These
other ideas—such as those attributing importance to altruism or
community—jostle for salience in the minds of the very same
citizens who also share the cynicism. Part of what I am trying to
do is to make a plea to others within the scholarly community
whose business it is to care, as a matter of scholarly concern,
about values—such as political scientists and philosophers—to join
vigorously in scholarly debate and instruction about public policy.

There is another sense in which this book has been an appeal
to put politics back into policy analysis. In addition to being concerned with who gets what and with what values people have,
politics also involves getting things done in a framework where
decisions are made by more than one person. It requires attention
to the views of others, to power, and to the process of decision
making—it requires, in a word, a strategy for trying to get accomplished what one would like to get accomplished. This appeal,
discussed in Chapter Four, has not been emphasized as deeply
in this book as have the philosophical concerns because it has
already received a great deal of attention among those who think

about and teach public policy; the view that one needs to be concerned with strategic issues is indeed a part of curricula in programs teaching public policy.

Economists who analyze regulatory policy have now gained, as a result of the 1980 elections, an unprecedented influence over the formation of public policy in areas such as environmental protection and occupational safety and health. The dominance of microeconomics in academic policy analysis now has its counterpart in a dominant role for practitioners of microeconomic analysis in actual policy formation. I suspect that unhappiness with some of the implications of various of the policies these practitioners plan to pursue will, slowly at first but gaining momentum over a period of time, produce a reaction. Just as many of the policies professed by the current administration were nurtured within the scholarly community and gradually became the stuff of practical politics, so too may the reaction to them first come within the world of ideas. Once developed there, it may move outward into the broader political debate.

Appendix

INTERVIEW QUESTIONS FOR ENVIRONMENTAL POLICY MAKERS

1. I'd like to start off by asking you how you got to your present job, and how long you've been at it?
2. (UNLESS MADE CLEAR FROM ANSWER TO QUESTION 1) What's your own background in terms of academic or professional training?
3. (FOR ENVIRONMENTALISTS AND CONGRESSIONAL STAFF ONLY) As we become more involved in something, we often develop additional reasons for seeing why what we are involved in is important. If you think back to the time *when you first became interested* in the environment, what considerations were dominant in your mind *then* in prompting your concern? (FOR STAFF) Or did you become involved in this area just because you got a job which required you to become involved?
4. (FOR INTEREST GROUPS ONLY) What would you say is the most important issue relating to environmental policy that your organization has worked on over the last few years?
5. (FOR INTEREST GROUPS ONLY) What are some other important issues relating to environmental quality that you've worked on over these last few years?
6. Are there any issues relating either to the protection of the environment or to the way the government goes about regulating environmental quality which, in your opinion, have not received the attention they deserve?
7. What criticisms, if any, would you make of the way we've gone about cleaning up the environment in the period since 1970?

8. One sometimes hears that it is hard for people involved in the day-to-day formulation of policy to take the time to consider policy alternatives or policy approaches different from those which come up in day-to-day legislative or agency battles. I'd like to ask you whether you happen to have any sources for getting information to learn about policy alternatives or policy approaches different from those which come up on a day-to-day basis? (PROBE: What are the sources?)

9. (IF YES) Are there any ideas you have come across for new directions or approaches or issues in environmental policy which you feel are worthy of serious consideration? (PROBE: What are they?)

10. (IF YES) Have you done anything personally to get such approaches/policies/issues considered by other people? (PROBE: What?)

11. Are there any (other) issues relating either to the protection of the environment or to the way the government goes about regulating environmental quality which in your opinion have not received the attention they deserve?

12. (FOR INTEREST GROUPS ONLY) Are there any specific provisions of our current environmental laws, or any entire laws, on which your organization took the initiative?

13. (IF YES) How did you come to perceive the problem?

14. (IF YES TO QUESTION 12) How did you go about getting the provision included in legislation/building support for the legislation?

(THE ORDERING ON THE QUESTIONS 15 AND 17 WILL BE REVERSED FOR HALF THE SAMPLE)

15. Some people say that we shouldn't be surprised that the environment is polluted too much, because traditionally polluting the environment has been free, and we do too much of anything that we don't have to pay for. Does that strike you as a good explanation for the pollution problem, or do you think there's much more to it than that?

16. (IF "MORE TO IT") What of importance does this explanation leave out?

17. Some people say that the fundamental reason the environment is polluted too much is that traditionally most individuals and industries have been too socially irresponsible, and not taken into account the effect of their actions on mankind and on our planet. Does that strike you as a good explanation for the pollution problem, or do you think there's much more to it than that?

18. (IF "MORE TO IT") What of importance does this explanation leave out?

19. Would you personally ever use the word "criminal" to describe the behavior of some individual or company that pollutes the environment?

20. (IF YES) Under what circumstances?
21. Do you think it is useful to use the word "blame" in reference to responsibility for pollution, or do you think that this is not a useful word? (PROBE: Why/why not?)
22. If you think of different sources of a given type of pollutant, is it your impression that different sources tend to face *relatively similar* costs in attaining a given degree of pollution abatement, *very different* costs, or don't you know enough about this to have an opinion?
23. (IF "VERY DIFFERENT COSTS") How would you go about dealing with this problem of differing costs?
24. There are times when EPA grants extended compliance schedules or other special conditions to firms which say they are having difficulties complying with environmental standards. There have been arguments made for and against such case-by-case adjustments. In general, do you think such case-by-case adjustments are a good thing?
25. (IF "NOT A GOOD THING") How would you go about dealing with the problem of special difficulties faced by some firms?
26. (FOR ENVIRONMENTALISTS AND STAFF ONLY) Sometimes the term "cost-effective" is used to describe one or another proposal made about dealing with pollution problems. When you hear the expression "cost-effective" used in connection with a proposal, does that term tend to make you more sympathetic to the proposal, less sympathetic, or doesn't it have any effect one way or another?
27. (IF "LESS SYMPATHETIC") Why is that?
28. Some air pollution state implementation plans allow for differential emissions reductions among different categories of sources of a given pollutant. That is, the plans may require one kind of source to reduce its emissions of, say, sulfur dioxide less than another kind of source is required to do. There have been arguments made for/against such variable emissions reduction requirements for various categories of sources. In general, do you think such variable emissions reduction requirements are a good thing? (PROBE: Why?)
29. For the rest of this interview, I'd like to ask you about one particular approach towards how to go about cleaning up the environment. Some people have recommended that, *instead of setting standards* for the discharge of pollutants into the air or water as we currently do, we should instead *place some sort of charge or tax* on discharges. In the field of water pollution control, these are sometimes called "effluent taxes," "effluent charges," or "effluent fees." For the sake of simplicity, I'm going to refer to these proposals as a "charges approach" towards pollution control.

    Let me start off by asking you this: Are you aware of the fact that such proposals for charges have been made in the area of water and air pollution? (IF NO, SKIP REST OF INTERVIEW.)

30. Could you explain why some people regard charges as superior to standards?

31. In your own view, what are the *advantages*, if any, of charges as over standards?

32. In your own view, what are the *disadvantages*, if any, of charges as over standards? (BE SURE TO PROBE HERE.)

33. All in all, do you think it would be a good idea to go over to using charges instead of standards, or not a good idea? (THIS QUESTION CAN BE ELIMINATED IF THE ANSWER IS OBVIOUS FROM ANSWERS TO PREVIOUS QUESTIONS.)

34. (FOR OPPONENTS ONLY) Often, people oppose various political positions because some other individual or group opposes the position, and we trust the judgment of that individual or group, or else we don't want to offend them. In the case of pollution charges, is there any individual or group whose opposition to charges is an important factor in your own opposition? (PROBE: Is that more because you trust his/their judgment, or more because you don't want to offend him/them?)

35. (UNLESS THIS ARGUMENT BROUGHT UP IN PREVIOUS ANSWERS TO PREVIOUS QUESTIONS) Proponents of charges argue that by using charges we could obtain a given degree of environmental quality for a lower cost than by using standards. Have you ever heard this argument for charges?

36. (IF YES) Could you explain on what basis people make this argument?

37. (FOR OPPONENTS OF CHARGES) Assuming it could be demonstrated to you that we could in fact obtain any given degree of environmental quality for 20% less cost to society using charges than by using standards, would this fact be sufficient to overcome your objections to a charges approach?

38. (IF NO) Why not?

39. (IF YES) (ENVIRONMENTALISTS AND STAFF ONLY) Let's say there's a one-in-ten chance that the critics are right, and that charges will work out worse than our current system of environmental regulation. That means there's a nine-in-ten chance that the proponents of charges are right, and that charges will allow the attainment of any given degree of environmental quality for 20% less cost. Do you think that the potential cost savings would be enough to outweigh the risks that charges won't work?

40. (UNLESS THIS ARGUMENT BROUGHT UP IN ANSWERS TO PREVIOUS QUESTIONS) Critics of charges sometimes argue that

industry will just pass the cost of any pollution charge along to consumers, and not reduce its pollution at all. Do you find this a convincing argument?

41. (IF YES, OR IF THIS ARGUMENT BROUGHT UP IN PREVIOUS QUESTIONS) (You argued earlier that industry would just pass the cost of any pollution charge to consumers.) The counterargument is that industry seeks to minimize its costs, and that if reducing pollution, and avoiding some of the charge, is cheaper than paying the charge, then industry will reduce the pollution. Do you find this counterargument convincing?

42. (IF NO) Why not?

43. (FOR ENVIRONMENTALISTS AND STAFF ONLY) Does it make any difference to you personally whether a company reduces its charges because society has said that such pollution is illegal, or because society has simply put a charge on pollution and so it becomes cheaper for companies to reduce pollution than to pay charges?

44. (FOR INDUSTRY AND STAFF ONLY) Do you think it would make any difference in terms of the credit the public gives industry for cleaning up the environment whether industry does this in response to government standards or to charges?

45. (IF YES) Why?

46. Let's assume a concrete proposal is made to introduce charges as a method of dealing with air or water pollution. Do you feel strongly enough for/against charges to spend any time working for/against such proposals?

47. (IF YES) What is it about the charges idea that makes you feel strongly enough about it to work for/against it?

48. (IF YES TO 46) Would you be willing to spend a good deal of time, or not much time, working for/against such a proposal?

49. (FOR OPPONENTS) Is there any group or individual who, by coming out for charges as a method of dealing with air or water pollution, would lead you to reconsider your opposition? (PROBE: Any others?)

50. (FOR OPPONENTS) Is there any new information you could imagine receiving which would make you change your point of view on charges?

51. (FOR SUPPORTERS) Is there any person or group whose support for charges would, in your opinion, make a decisive difference in the success of these proposals?

52. (FOR SUPPORTERS) Do you have any ideas about why a charges approach has not gotten further than it has?

53. If a charges proposal were introduced, whom would you expect its major supporters to be?

54. What about its major opponents?
55. Has anyone ever spoken to you trying to persuade you to support a charges approach to environmental regulation?
56. (IF YES) How did you react to this person/these people?
57. Have you ever read any material advocating a charges approach?
58. Since you first heard a charges approach advocated, has your opinion towards it changed at all? (PROBE: In what direction?)
59. Do you happen to know what position, if any, Senator Muskie and Leon Billings take on using charges as a tool of environmental regulation? (PROBE: What is it?)

THE REMAINING QUESTIONS ARE FOR ENVIRONMENTAL-ISTS AND CONGRESSIONAL STAFF ONLY:

60. Finally, some of the transportation control programs EPA has considered over the years involve parking surcharges for cars parked or driven in polluted urban areas. Other proposals involve direct restrictions on driving in these areas. In general, which of these two approaches do you feel is a better way to go? (PROBE: Why?)
61. Let's say that a parking surcharge, developed as part of a transportation control program, reflects the costs a driver imposes on society by driving a car, including the damages from auto pollution. If the surcharge reflects all such costs, would you then feel it was OK for a person to drive his car in the city center as long as he paid the surcharge, or would you still criticize him for not taking available public transportation?
62. I would like to talk a bit about proposals for product charges for materials that can enter the solid waste stream. As you know, proposals have been made to levy product charges on packaging materials such as beverage bottles, paper, and so forth. In general, are you sympathetic to such proposals or not sympathetic?
63. There have also been proposals made to regulate packaging which is excessive from a solid waste point of view. How would you compare that idea with the product charge idea?
64. (FOR OPPONENTS OF AIR/WATER CHARGES, BUT SUP-PORTERS OF SOLID WASTE CHARGES) Is there anything which makes you sympathetic to the idea of using charges to deal with solid waste problems, at the same time that you are unsympathetic to using them to deal with air or water pollution?
65. Let's say that a charge is added onto packaging materials that reflects the damage that such materials cause society—including both the costs of disposal and the aesthetic damage litter causes. If such a charge were to reflect all the damage, would you then feel that if

a consumer wishes to buy the packaging and pay the extra cost, it is OK for him to do so, or would you still criticize such a consumer for being wasteful?

66. It has been proposed that, as part of an eventual product charge on packaging material, there be some rebate on recycled material to reflect the fact that it uses fewer resources and that it places fewer demands on our solid waste disposal systems. Let's say that a rebate is established for recycled material which reflects these social advantages of using it. What if anything, would you favor doing if such a rebate did not succeed in making recycled material significantly more competitive with virgin material?

INDEX